Grades 2–5

NONFICTION WRITING
LESSONS THAT WORK

Engaging Ways to Help Students Plan and Write Informational Texts

LOLA M. SCHAEFER

■SCHOLASTIC

New York • Toronto • London • Auckland • Sydney
Mexico City • New Delhi • Hong Kong • Buenos Aires

Dedication

For all the teachers who constantly seek stronger writing instruction, thank you for your dedication and commitment. Enjoy the journey with your students.

—LMS

Cover design: Jorge J. Namerow
Cover photograph: © iStock
Interior design: Sarah Morrow
Development Editor: Joanna Davis-Swing
Editor: Sarah Glasscock

ISBN: 978-0-545-27350-3
Copyright © 2012 by Lola M. Schaefer
All rights reserved.
Printed in the U.S.A.

1 2 3 4 5 6 7 8 9 10   40   19 18 17 16 15 14 13 12

Contents

Introduction

Writing is thinking. It requires reflection on focused content and organization, word choice and sentence structure, development of ideas, and even the mechanics. When students write, the pace of the school day slows down. They need time to consider what it is they want to say and how to say it.

So it only makes sense that teachers provide many opportunities for students to write in the different content areas. If we want optimum comprehension of historical data, social issues, mathematical concepts, biographical information, and scientific cycles and processes, we need to ask students to show us what they know by writing.

In the past, there were only two kinds of factual writing happening in schools— answering questions at the end of textbook chapters and writing the required research report. Both kinds of writing carry expectations that students will read respectable sources of information and regurgitate the information with textbook language and accuracy.

When I was an elementary school student, these were the only two means that I ever used to prove to my teachers that I "knew the material." I probably answered thousands of end-of-chapter questions with the precision of a robot, and I wrote at least four research reports a year in grades 3–8. I wrote about dead presidents, dead inventors, dead explorers, and the occasional mountain range or national landmark. I was given a topic by the teacher, read parts of two or three library books, plus an encyclopedic entry or two, then wrote a three-, four-, or five-page report using expository prose.

I can't remember any of the topics of these reports. Once, though, as an adult, I recognized a photograph of Rutherford B. Hayes, so I imagine that one of the presidential assignments was about him. The reason I can't recall who or what I wrote about is that it wasn't important to me. An educational precept of the era was that researching, outlining, and writing factual reports would prepare me for more difficult work in high school and college. And maybe it did; I don't know. All I do know is that I would always hurry and get those "papers" completed so I could read a good chapter book, which I would have sitting on the corner of my desk.

And still, today, I'll walk into a school and see 100+ third-grade animal reports stapled to the wall. They all begin with the name of the animal, its natural habitat, a list of foods it likes to eat, perhaps the names of its predators and the defense mechanism it uses to escape, along with its expected lifespan. Each report has the same format. And I always wonder how long it took these students to write their reports and whether they were truly engaged during the process. I have my suspicions.

I also see teachers offering choices to students. During the year, they expose students to many kinds of informational and nonfiction writing (see the next section for a definition of each kind of writing). Students are allowed to self-select topics and narrow those topics to focused writing ideas. They also select the text structure that will highlight the information they want to share. These classrooms are filled with enthusiasm and energy. Students are highly engaged and committed to their work.

That's the kind of climate we want for all children—a room where purpose, audience, and the focus of the content drive their choices. We want a learning community where children think about the interrelationships among the facts they read and the implications of these facts in the world at large. We want students to be able to use the features of nonfiction text—glossaries, indexes, tables of contents, and sidebars—when they are researching. But more important, we want students to be able to read facts, blend new information with what they already know, and decide how they want to share what they consider important with others.

My observations have shown me that when students write in a given content area and select their own text structures, they are more committed to writing accurately. They return to their sources several times to check dates, names, drawings, events, graphs, or diagrams, and when they do, they often notice details that they did not see initially. They are now reading like thinkers and writers. They might recognize a passage on the serrations of shark teeth or how the length of a butterfly's proboscis determines the amount of nectar it can sip at once. As students' engagement increases, their sense of purpose as they read and their level of attention to detail also increases.

Why Is It Important to Teach Informational and Nonfiction Writing?

In schools today, "informational text" refers to both true informational writing and nonfiction text types. Nell Duke, an educator and literacy researcher, defines informational text as "text written with the primary purpose of conveying information about the natural and social world (typically from someone presumed to be more knowledgeable on the subject to someone presumed to be less so) and having particular text features to accomplish this purpose. Features commonly found in informational texts include graphic elements, such as diagrams and photographs; text structures, such as compare/contrast and cause and effect" (p. 1, 2003).

A good example of informational text is the book *A Seed Is Sleepy* by Dianna Hutts Aston. The author shows many of the characteristics of seeds, from how they travel to the fruits they bear. Another instance of informational text is *Pond Circle* by Betsy Franco, in which the food web of a pond is depicted through a cumulative tale.

In contrast, nonfiction text usually tells about a historical event, a famous person, how to do something, or facts about a topic. An example of nonfiction writing is the picture book biography *Snowflake Bentley* by Jacqueline Briggs Martin. *A Drop of Water* by Walter Wick is a nonfiction book that examines the molecular makeup of water, surface tension, and many other aspects of water, from frost to dew to snowflakes.

Informational and nonfiction texts are both valuable resources for facts and knowledge. In order to excite and inspire students, teachers need to provide both types of text in their classrooms, offering students a choice of how to show what they know in their content areas.

Writing across the curriculum builds comprehension of the material in the content areas, and it offers another opportunity for students to practice and stretch their writing skills. Informational and nonfiction writing also do the following:

- provide a purpose for research
- offer students the opportunity to make sense of their research
- help students see the relationships, interdependence, and contrasts in what they study
- show students how their new learning connects with their prior knowledge
- show teachers what students understand and what they don't
- integrate content areas in a meaningful way for students

It is important that students have the opportunity to write informational and nonfiction text so they can learn about the world around them, past and present, and imagine and prepare for the future.

Choice

When students have a choice of what topic to study, it increases their level of commitment to writing. So does having the choice of form or structure. Give students a choice of three or four different informational or nonfiction structures and then allow them to select the one that matches their writing purpose.

Even when you are introducing students to a new text structure, give them choice. Show them two or three books, each with a different format. Ask one student to select the structure to explore for that day. The more choice we offer students, the more responsibility they will assume for making independent choices in the future.

Effective Writing Instruction

As with all writing, informational and nonfiction texts require that students be supported with solid instruction as they write. Begin by showing examples from mentor texts. Take time with this literature and ask questions that help students "read like a writer." Continue the process by helping them brainstorm topics, not only in language arts class but also while you're teaching science, social studies, math, and reading. Encourage students to keep their writers' notebooks on the corner of their desks, so topics of interest can be quickly entered.

Purpose

Remind students *why* they are writing informational or nonfiction text. The purpose can be to inform, to explain, to share WOW! facts, and even to entertain an audience. Who will their audience be? A writer needs to decide this before deciding on a format or choosing words or sentence structure. If the intended audience is first graders, then the sentence structure will be simpler than it would be for peers or seventh graders.

Modeling

Modeling is one of the strongest tools a teacher has. Show students how to select a topic by brainstorming with them. Model each step of the prewrite so students understand the organization of the text structure. As you work through a prewrite, either allow time for students to record this planning step in their writer's notebook or post a sample of the prewrite so they can refer to the format and features. Continue by modeling how to use reminder words from the prewriting plan to construct detailed sentences that will engage their audience and share the intended meaning.

Some collaborative writing is necessary when introducing new structures in grades 2–5, but once this groundwork has been done, students need to work independently. Think of your modeling as a scaffold that provides tools so students can express themselves more effectively.

Mini-Lessons

Mini-lessons on craft strengthen students' informational and nonfiction writing. Besides the usual mini-lessons on focus, word choice, details and development, punctuation, grammar, and spelling, it's important to provide mini-lessons that show the difference between known facts and WOW! facts—facts an audience will want to read or hear. For example, as this chart demonstrates, general facts about sharks are not nearly as compelling as WOW! facts.

General Facts	WOW! Facts
Many sharks live in oceans.	More than 350 different kinds of sharks swim in the oceans.
A shark has a lot of sharp teeth in its mouth.	A shark has nearly 3,000 teeth in its mouth.
Sharks eat other sea creatures.	Sharks use their teeth to rip and tear their prey into bite-size pieces. But they do not chew their food once it is in their mouth.

Finally, provide opportunities for your students to share their informational or nonfiction writing with an audience. Show them how to use questions to prepare readers or listeners to provide helpful feedback. Find pockets of time for their audience to respond. Without feedback, students lose their drive and commitment to write, and to write better.

What Tools Does This Book Provide?

This book offers teachers practical text structures that appeal to students and help them show what they know, regardless of subject matter. However, all of the writing discussed in this book has one requirement: it must contain accurate facts. Students must understand that the purpose of informational or nonfiction text is to offer a given audience real facts about the real world. That can never be compromised.

Each chapter includes the following:

- an exploration of a particular text structure

- recommendations for published literature that offer examples of the text structure

- a guided lesson in which students write an example of the text structure collaboratively

- ways to encourage students to self-select topics

- the purpose of the text structure

- a process for encouraging students' independent writing, including elements of craft

- audience/feedback suggestions

Writing instruction is a blend of genre and craft, so I've listed the elements of craft associated with each particular writing structure in every chapter. This way, you can offer mini-lessons on those craft elements while students are writing in that form.

Underlying this book is the idea that most teachers will start by introducing shorter pieces of informational and nonfiction text. The shorter pieces are stepping stones that build stamina and skill in the student writers so they can manage larger pieces more easily.

Finally, Common Core State Standards (CCSS) include a significant emphasis on informational writing. Not all school districts agree, though, on what constitutes strong informational writing. What we do know is that all educators and parents want students to be able to write factual information in a way that engages an audience and reflects learning. The chart below shows the correlation between the chapters in this book and the CCSS.

Correlation of Text Structures to Common Core State Standards (CCSS)

GRADE 2

TEXT TYPES AND PURPOSES

W.2.2.   Write informative/explanatory texts in which they introduce a topic, use facts and definitions to develop points, and provide a concluding statement or section. (*Chapters 2, 4, 6*)

W.2.3.   Write narratives in which they recount a well-elaborated event or short sequence of events, include details to describe actions, thoughts, and feelings, use temporal words to signal event order, and provide a sense of closure. (*Chapter 7*)

PRODUCTION AND DISTRIBUTION OF WRITING

W.2.5. With guidance and support from adults and peers, focus on a topic and strengthen writing as needed by revising and editing. (*Chapters 2–8*)

W.2.6. With guidance and support from adults, use a variety of digital tools to produce and publish writing, including in collaboration with peers. (*Chapters 2–8*)

RESEARCH TO BUILD AND PRESENT KNOWLEDGE

W.2.7. Participate in shared research and writing projects (e.g., read a number of books on a single topic to produce a report; record science observations). (*Chapters 2–8*)

W.2.8. Recall information from experiences or gather information from provided sources to answer a question. (*Chapters 2–8*)

GRADE 3

TEXT TYPES AND PURPOSES

W.3.2. Write informative/explanatory texts to examine a topic and convey ideas and information clearly. (*Chapters 2, 4, 6*)

- Introduce a topic and group related information together; include illustrations when useful to aid comprehension.
- Develop the topic with facts, definitions, and details.
- Use linking words and phrases (e.g., *also, another, and, more, but*) to connect ideas within categories of information.
- Provide a concluding statement or section.

W.3.3. Write narratives to develop real or imagined experiences or events using effective technique, descriptive details, and clear event sequences. (*Chapter 7*)

- Establish a situation and introduce a narrator and/or characters; organize an event sequence that unfolds naturally.
- Use dialogue and descriptions of actions, thoughts, and feelings to develop experiences and events or show the response of characters to situations.
- Use temporal words and phrases to signal event order.
- Provide a sense of closure.

PRODUCTION AND DISTRIBUTION OF WRITING

W.3.4. With guidance and support from adults, produce writing in which the development and organization are appropriate to task and purpose. (*Chapters 2–8*)

W.3.5. With guidance and support from peers and adults, develop and strengthen writing as needed by planning, revising, and editing. (*Chapters 2–8*)

W.3.6. With guidance and support from adults, use technology to produce and publish writing (using keyboarding skills) as well as to interact and collaborate with others. (*Chapters 2–8*)

RESEARCH TO BUILD AND PRESENT KNOWLEDGE

W.3.7. Conduct short research projects that build knowledge about a topic. (*Chapters 2–8*)

W.3.8. Recall information from experiences or gather information from print and digital sources; take brief notes on sources and sort evidence into provided categories. (*Chapters 2–8*)

RANGE OF WRITING

W.3.10. Write routinely over extended time frames (time for research, reflection, and revision) and shorter time frames (a single sitting or a day or two) for a range of discipline-specific tasks, purposes, and audiences. (*Chapters 2–8*)

GRADE 4

TEXT TYPES AND PURPOSES

W.4.2. Write informative/explanatory texts to examine a topic and convey ideas and information clearly. (*Chapters 2, 4, 6*)

- Introduce a topic clearly and group related information in paragraphs and sections.

- Develop the topic with facts, definitions, concrete details, quotations, or other information and examples related to the topic.

W.4.3. Write narratives to develop real or imagined experiences or events using effective technique, descriptive details, and clear event sequences. (*Chapter 7*)

- Orient the reader by establishing a situation and introducing a narrator and/or characters; organize an event sequence that unfolds naturally.

- Use dialogue and description to develop experiences and events or show the responses of characters to situations.

- Use a variety of transitional words and phrases to manage the sequence of events.

- Use concrete words and phrases and sensory details to convey experiences and events precisely.

- Provide a conclusion that follows from the narrated experiences or events.

PRODUCTION AND DISTRIBUTION OF WRITING

W.4.4. Produce clear and coherent writing in which the development and organization are appropriate to task, purpose, and audience. (*Chapters 2–8*)

W.4.5. With guidance and support from peers and adults, develop and strengthen writing as needed by planning, revising, and editing. (*Chapters 2–8*)

W.4.6. With some guidance and support from adults, use technology, including the Internet, to produce and publish writing as well as to interact and collaborate with

Nonfiction Writing Lessons That Work © 2012 by Lola M. Schaefer, Scholastic Teaching Resources

others; demonstrate sufficient command of keyboarding skills to type a minimum of one page in a single sitting. (*Chapters 2–8*)

RESEARCH TO BUILD AND PRESENT KNOWLEDGE

W.4.7. Conduct short research projects that build knowledge through investigation of different aspects of a topic. (*Chapters 2–8*)

W.4.8. Recall relevant information from experiences or gather relevant information from print and digital sources. (*Chapters 2–8*)

W.4.9. Draw evidence from literary or informational texts to support analysis, reflection, and research. (*Chapters 2–8*)

- Apply *grade 4 Reading standards* to literature (e.g., "Describe in depth a character, setting, or event in a story or drama, drawing on specific details in the text (e.g., a character's thoughts, words, or actions).").

- Apply *grade 4 Reading standards* to informational texts (e.g., "Explain how an author uses reasons and evidence to support particular points in a text").

RANGE OF WRITING

W.4.10. Write routinely over extended time frames (time for research, reflection, and revision) and shorter time frames (a single sitting or a day or two) for a range of discipline-specific tasks, purposes, and audiences. (*Chapters 2–8*)

GRADE 5

TEXT TYPES AND PURPOSES

W.5.2. Write informative/explanatory texts to examine a topic and convey ideas and information clearly. (*Chapters 2, 4, 6*)

- Introduce a topic clearly, provide a general observation and focus, and group related information logically.

- Develop the topic with facts, definitions, concrete details, quotations, or other information and examples related to the topic.

W.5.3. Write narratives to develop real or imagined experiences or events using effective technique, descriptive details, and clear event sequences. (*Chapter 7*)

- Orient the reader by establishing a situation and introducing a narrator and/or characters; organize an event sequence that unfolds naturally.

- Use narrative techniques, such as dialogue, description, and pacing, to develop experiences and events or show the responses of characters to situations.

- Use a variety of transitional words, phrases, and clauses to manage the sequence of events.

- Use concrete words and phrases and sensory details to convey experiences and events precisely.

- Provide a conclusion that follows from the narrated experiences or events.

PRODUCTION AND DISTRIBUTION OF WRITING

W.5.4. Produce clear and coherent writing in which the development and organization are appropriate to task, purpose, and audience. (*Chapters 2–8*)

W.5.5. With guidance and support from peers and adults, develop and strengthen writing as needed by planning, revising, editing, rewriting, or trying a new approach. (*Chapters 2–8*)

W.5.6. With some guidance and support from adults, use technology, including the Internet, to produce and publish writing as well as to interact and collaborate with others; demonstrate sufficient command of keyboarding skills to type a minimum of two pages in a single sitting. (*Chapters 2–8*)

RESEARCH TO BUILD AND PRESENT KNOWLEDGE

W.5.7. Conduct short research projects that use several sources to build knowledge through investigation of different aspects of a topic. (*Chapters 2–8*)

W.5.8. Recall relevant information from experiences or gather relevant information from print and digital sources. (*Chapters 2–8*)

W.5.9. Draw evidence from literary or informational texts to support analysis, reflection, and research. (*Chapters 2–8*)

- Apply *grade 5 Reading standards* to literature (e.g., "Compare and contrast two or more characters, settings, or events in a story or a drama, drawing on specific details in the text (e.g., how characters interact)").

- Apply *grade 5 Reading standards* to informational texts (e.g., "Explain how an author uses reasons and evidence to support particular points in a text, identifying which reasons and evidence support which point(s)").

RANGE OF WRITING

W.5.10. Write routinely over extended time frames (time for research, reflection, and revision) and shorter time frames (a single sitting or a day or two) for a range of discipline-specific tasks, purposes, and audiences. (*Chapters 2–8*)

Informational and nonfiction writing can be one of the most exciting experiences for students in your classroom. They become engaged while learning facts about the real world. When students find new information intriguing or captivating, they are eager to share it with others. Provide the tools and modeling, then sit back and watch your students write with purpose and joy. You'll be amazed by what they will show you that they know.

CHAPTER 1

Organizing to Show What You Know

Many teachers tell me that they avoid informational or nonfiction writing because their students copy, or plagiarize, from reference materials. This book offers processes and structures that emphasize thinking about content and reorganizing facts. We want students to be engaged by what they read about the real world. We want to encourage their interest in and fascination with factual information. We want students to take that knowledge and fuse it with what they already know when they produce informational or nonfiction writing.

It's important to help students select the kind of informational and nonfiction structures that will match their topics and intentions. One way we can do this is by providing an assortment of mentor texts that expose students to a wide variety of text structures. Children's literature is rich with examples of historical journals, cumulative tales of the cycles in nature, compare and contrast, cause and effect, terse verse, informational poetry, science and math riddles, real-life stories, and actual-size books. Once we show students the many possibilities, it is easier for them to choose a text structure that matches the content of their writing.

I've seen teachers ask students who are studying westward expansion to become a pioneer and write in a journal for three or four days. The only requirement is that students include factual information in the journal entries. For instance, if a student wrote about homesteading west of the Mississippi River, then she might include a scene that describes the devastation to crops from drought, flooding, or grasshoppers. If a student were keeping a diary told from the perspective of an apprentice to Paul Revere, he would need to include facts about the secret meetings of the Sons of Liberty or the taxes that were being imposed on the colonists. This is a form of writing that forces students to synthesize what they have learned about historical periods into what they already know about daily life and human behavior. No copying can take place.

I've also seen students describe the life cycle of a frog or a monarch butterfly using the cumulative tale structure. Was the students' information accurate? You bet! And because of the form, there is no way that students could copy any of the factual information in the writing from a book. Instead, they needed to understand the different developmental stages of the frog or butterfly and shape that knowledge into the cumulative form.

I enjoy asking students to design a memorial for a famous person whom they have studied. This requires writers to make informed choices about the following:

- the location of the memorial
- the type of memorial (coin, statue, wall, bridge, frieze, fountain, and so on)
- the materials used to construct the memorial
- its shape or design
- any quotes or words that will appear on the memorial
- any symbols that might appear on it
- its purpose
- its size

Students must make all these choices with the subject in mind. For instance, a memorial for the Wright Brothers would not be made from crystal; their working lives were far removed from this kind of finery. Instead, their memorial might be constructed from wood and canvas, much like their first plane—the Flyer. It wouldn't be located in San Francisco—the Wright Brothers probably never even visited that part of the country. It would be located either in Dayton, Ohio, near the site of their original bicycle shop, or at Kitty Hawk, North Carolina, where they made their first flights.

Once again, no copying or plagiarism is possible here because the design of the memorial is totally generated by the student. He might refer back to resources to check dates or how one glider developed into another, but copying sentences would not help develop the memorial.

There is only one informational or nonfiction structure that encourages copying: the research report.

The Research Report

As I mentioned earlier, when I visit schools, I usually see a number of reports hanging in the halls. Quite often, when I stop and read them on the way to classrooms, I notice that each one has the same structure, the same general topic, and they all, more or less, answer the same questions. I read five, six, or seven different papers, trying to find one example of a student who wrote something that was important to him or her, one student who was bold enough to use his or her own organization. I search for a single instance in which the author deviated just a bit from the template and included self-selected information. Instead, I read clones. The reports contain no misspelled words, no grammatical errors, and no missing punctuation, but unfortunately they contain nothing of interest—nothing to engage the reader.

I understand that most teachers wrote reports when they were in school. There's a comfort in teaching something that we mastered as students ourselves. However, research and practice has taken the educational world beyond this formulaic writing. The writing experience for students in grades 2–5 needs to involve reading, thinking, deliberate word selection, and drafting. Students need an opportunity to receive feedback, and genuine learning must take place.

The different structures presented in this book will take your students deeper into their informational and nonfiction reading. They will initiate conversations about what is factual and what isn't. They will take care in their selection of WOW! facts or other important information to share with an audience. Their writing will have relevance.

For a quick comparison, study the lists on the next two pages. One describes a typical report assigned in many elementary classrooms. The other lists the benefits of having students choose a text structure that matches the factual information they would like to share.

If you work in a school system that requires students to write at least one research report each year, make that experience as authentic as you can. The following process will make writing this report engaging for your students:

- **Allow self-selection of topic.** Students can either choose something that they already know a lot about, or they can select a topic that they would like to research.

- **Depending on the age of your students, ask them to narrow their focus.** One way to do this is to have each writer select one aspect of the topic to write about in detail. For instance, a student might choose to write about a giraffe's neck. She might include information about the size, the number of muscles in its neck, the amount of time it takes a giraffe to swallow food, how its neck helps the giraffe reach leaves at the tops of trees, and so on. Another way to help students narrow a topic is to have them make a list of 4–8 questions they would like to answer in their reports. Encourage them to present that information in the same way they would share it if they were speaking in front of a class of younger students. What would the audience need to know first, second, third, and so on?

- **Remind students that research simply confirms or informs them of facts** but that you would like them to only write reminder words when researching. Later they will develop those words into detailed sentences.

- **Allow students to return to reference materials to confirm dates, events, or facts.** Continually remind them that they must have a purpose for their report writing. Tell them to consider these questions: *What is it I want to share with my audience? Why is that important? Is it factual information? How will I organize this information?* Once your students have selected a topic and purpose, they will be able to write a meaningful report that will engage readers.

Traditional Report

Topic: teacher-selected or randomly selected by students

Purpose: to research and find answers to specific questions about topic

Structure: teacher-provided, formal writing

Prewrite: often a list of sentences copied from a textbook, an encyclopedia, or an online source

Content: teacher-guided

Process: teacher-driven

Audience: teacher

Feedback: grade and/or teacher comments

Authentic Informational or Nonfiction Writing of Choice

Topic: student-selected and focused

Purpose: to share factual information that the student finds interesting and would be appealing to an audience

Structure: student-selected, matches style and tone of content

Prewrite: matches the structure of the writing and requires synthesis of information

Content: student-selected

Process: student-driven

Audience: student, peers, and teacher

Feedback: authentic from peers, self-evaluation

CHAPTER 2

Show With Informational Sidebars

As students study new information, they always find some facts that wow them. I encourage you to celebrate that enthusiasm by showing them how to write sidebars, which are short (typically three or four sentences) and highly focused forms of writing.

Exploring Informational Sidebars

Materials: a collection of sidebars from different sources, including textbooks, published literature, magazine articles, and brochures

Begin by showing students 7–10 sidebars you've collected. Examine the sidebars thoroughly, then return to one and reread it again. A sample sidebar appears below:

A professional basketball court measures 94 feet long and 50 feet wide. The top of the rim of the basket is 10 feet off the ground. The free throw line is 15 feet from the backboard.

Engage students in a discussion of the sidebar, such as the following:

Teacher: What kind of a sidebar is this? Is the information . . .

- biographical (detailed information about a person)?

- statistical (providing specific numbers or data)?

- historical (details about an event or a place)?

Literature Links

These picture books include sidebars to convey information:

- Animal Dads
  by Sneed B. Collard III

- An Egg Is Quiet
  by Dianna Aston

- The Flag We Love
  by Pam Muñoz Ryan

- Meet the Howlers
  by April Pulley Sayre

- A Seed Is Sleepy
  by Dianna Aston

- William Shakespeare & the Globe
  by Aliki

- a timeline?

- explanatory (how something is accomplished or built)?

- a graph or diagram?

- descriptive?

- another kind of information?

Most students will say that the sample sidebar describes the dimensions of a basketball court or is statistical because it gives exact measurements.

Repeat this same process with the entire class for another three or four sidebars.

Independent Student Work

For additional practice, ask students to look through their textbooks or informational texts from the library and find a sidebar. After a few students read aloud their sidebars, ask them to describe the kind of information it includes.

Allow students to categorize the sidebar they chose in their own language. The label is not as important as having them think about the purpose of this type of writing.

Looking again at the first sidebar you introduced, ask, "So why do you think the author chose to add this information?" Provide an opportunity for students to explain the author's intent in their own words. For example, some students might say that the sample sidebar shows that there are exact measurements for a basketball court. Others might say it shows that these dimensions are for the professional court and that there might be others for high school or college basketball courts.

To help students think deeper about the author's intent, ask, "Who would want to know this information?" We want students to think about how we craft writing to appeal to a specific group of people or to a general audience. In response to the sample sidebar, a student might answer that anyone interested in the game of basketball would be interested in the size of the court. Another student might say that this information would be helpful to someone planning to build a basketball court.

Then ask, "Is this sidebar easy to understand?" Guide students to examine the language and how the information is presented. For instance, since this sample sidebar is so straightforward, students will probably say that it is quite easy to understand the information.

Focus is the last part of this examination. Ask, "What factual information did the author offer the reader with this sidebar? How many different facts can you find?" We always want students to realize that sidebars contain facts—real information about the real world. Regarding the sample sidebar above, a student might say that it focuses solely on the actual size or dimensions of the basketball court.

Sidebars on Display

Create a small bulletin board with copies of sidebars from textbooks, magazines, nonfiction or informational picture books, brochures, and manuals. Each day, read two sidebars aloud and ask students to categorize them. One student can then label the sidebars that you've discussed. In this way, students have concrete examples before their eyes. This support will help them include different kinds of information in their own writing.

Writing Sidebars

Materials: a short, interesting print or online article, an interactive whiteboard or overhead projector

The first time your students write sidebars needs to be a collaborative effort, so they are supported throughout the process.

Begin by brainstorming topics that all your students care about. Once you decide on a topic, find a short but interesting article in a magazine, or download a posting from a reputable online source, such as Enchanted Learning (*www.enchantedlearning.com*). Display the article and read it out loud once. Then initiate a discussion like the one modeled below, which focuses on an article about hammerhead sharks:

Teacher: I'm going to read this article again. Stop me when you hear a WOW!

[*Underline the WOW! facts that students mention.*]

The first fact we underlined was about the size and weight of a hammerhead shark. We also underlined information about what these sharks eat; how they use their hammer-shaped head to hold their prey; a description of their sharp, serrated teeth; how their teeth rip and tear; and how these sharks can birth 20–340 pups that are approximately 27 inches long. You found quite a few interesting facts. Who would like to read our first underlined fact? What is that fact about? What is its focus?

Liam: The sharks' size.

Teacher: Please write "size" above that fact. Now, go ahead and read the next fact.

[*After each fact, ask the student to identify the focus and write that word or phrase above the information so everyone can see it easily.*]

Teacher: Many of these facts are focused on one aspect of the sharks' lives. What aspect is that?

Sachi: What and how sharks eat.

Teacher: Let's make that our focus and write a sidebar with WOW! facts.

Finding a Focus

If students struggle to identify the focus of most of the underlined facts, color-code the information. For instance, if students are creating a sidebar about an animal, ask them to highlight any WOW! facts as follows: size (green), food or eating behaviors (blue), habitat (yellow), enemies or defense mechanisms (orange), life cycle (red), and so on. Then ask, "Which color has the most facts?" Students will then identify the major grouping of one color. Make that category the focus of the sidebar.

Teacher: Many sidebars, but not all, have a title that gives readers a clue as to what they will be reading. Let's think of some choices for a title for our sidebar on what and how a hammerhead shark eats. Try and think of titles that will grab your readers' attention and make them want to read more. I'll start. How about "Food for Thought," "Come and Get It," "Undersea Feast," or "What's for Dinner?"

[*As you call out your suggestions, write them on the board or a chart so all students can see them.*]

What are your suggestions?

Lucas: "Food. Food. Food."

Lorraine: "How Hammerheads Eat."

Max: "Watch Out!"

Keisha: "What Sharp Teeth You Have."

Spencer: "Dinnertime."

Teacher: These are all exceptional titles. Which one has some zip, gives the reader a hint of what the sidebar is going to be about, and would make the audience want to read on?

[*Don't take a vote. Simply call on one student to make a choice for the class.*]

Riley: "What Sharp Teeth You Have."

Teacher: Great choice! Let's all write that at the top of our sheet of paper. Or, if you prefer one of our other choices, write that title.

Return to your list of facts. Through discussion, decide which of the facts to include in the sidebar. Then ask one student to come forward and number those facts in the order that makes the most sense. Write the first sentence in the sidebar; students may copy it. Then say, "Now that we have the first sentence, I want you to finish the sidebar on your own. Decide how to include these facts. Remember, a sidebar is informative, and it is also engaging for the reader. Make sure your writing pops on the page."

Continue this process until students have written the facts in their own words. As students write their sidebars, write your own, but out of their sight. Provide time for partner-sharing, and then ask two or three students to read their sidebars to the entire class. Be sure that you show your sidebar and read it, too.

Self-Selected Topics for Sidebars

When students select their own topics, they become more committed to their research and to the process of writing a fact-based sidebar. Plus, it's more interesting and fun for students to share what they've written if everyone has taken a different topic and focus.

As students complete a unit of study in science, social studies, or even math, encourage them to record some WOW! facts. For instance, if you're studying space, one student might want to write a sidebar on sunspots, another on what the rings of Saturn are made of, while someone else might focus on the distances between planets.

If your students maintain individual writer's notebooks, then they will have an ongoing list of topics they want to explore through writing. They might research a topic that they've always wondered about or one they've only begun to learn about in class.

The Purpose Behind Writing Sidebars

Writing sidebars accomplishes quite a few classroom goals. It provides an opportunity for students to share what excites them in their learning. It teaches them how to keep a tight focus on a topic and develop just one idea. Sidebars can be completed quickly, and the activity serves as a great precursor to other forms of informational and nonfiction writing because the emphasis is on focus and facts.

Process for Independent Writing
Review the steps for writing a sidebar with students:
✓ Select a topic of interest.
✓ Research that topic for WOW! facts.
✓ Select 5 or 6 facts that would engage an audience.
✓ Select 2 or 3 facts to focus on. Decide on the order for presenting the facts.
✓ If you want to include a title for your sidebar, brainstorm three to five choices. Select the title that will grab readers' attention, provide a hint about the topic, and make readers want to read on.
✓ Write the factual information in your own words so that it pops on the page.

 Nonfiction Writing Lessons That Work © 2012 by Lola M. Schaefer, Scholastic Teaching Resources

THE ELEMENTS OF CRAFT

Students practice the following elements of craft while writing informational sidebars: focus, word choice, details and development, voice and conventions.

You can design mini-lessons on any or all of these to improve the quality of the writing.

Sidebar Samples

As extra support for your students, post sample sidebars in your classroom. The more students can study the structure, the more successful they will be. Here are some examples:

OUCH!

Stay away from the tail of a scorpion. Why? That's the end that could sting you. A telson—a small, pouch-like body part—contains two glands that make venom. A sharp barb on the outside of the telson injects venom into the scorpion's enemy.

The venom hurts.

_____

In 1492, most people thought the earth was the center of the universe, and the sun and stars moved around it. Not Leonardo da Vinci. He wrote notes that read, "The Sun Does Not Move." Very few people believed his idea.

_____

Zeugen? What's That?

A zeugen can be found in desert lands. It's a table-shaped formation made when high winds erode the softer rock underneath. The upper rock remains because it is much harder and wind-resistant.

_____

Every day, the world produces approximately 9,000 tons of cocoa beans. Those beans can make 720 million chocolate bars. YUM.

Audience/Feedback

Provide at least 3–5 opportunities for students to write informational sidebars. These do not have to be published, but some students may choose to edit and publish one of their favorites. However, it is important for all writers to receive feedback on their efforts. To do this, have student pairs read their sidebars to each other.

A few suggestions for partner sharing are shown below. Select only one suggestion for each partner share.

- Listen carefully and then tell the author which two facts you most enjoyed hearing.

- Listen carefully and then tell the writer what you believe the focus of his or her sidebar was.

- Listen carefully and then tell the author why you think that he or she chose that particular title.

- Listen carefully and then tell the writer the one fact that you thought contained WOW! information.

Nonfiction Writing Lessons That Work © 2012 by Lola M. Schaefer, Scholastic Teaching Resources

CHAPTER 3

Show Facts With Terse Verse

"Terse verse" is a term that describes two-word sentences: *Terse* because it's short and abrupt; *verse* because it's written in couplets. Some terse verse will rhyme and some will not. I typically encourage students to forget the rhyme and concentrate on meaning. This is an accessible informational format that guides students to think more deeply about topics they are studying in math, social studies, and science.

Exploring Terse Verse

Materials: a collection of books containing examples of terse verse (see the Literature Link); an interactive whiteboard, overhead projector, or other form of display

Begin by reading an example of terse verse to your students. Show how the author used strong, specific nouns and verbs to convey the meaning. Copy a couple of the lines from the book and display them.

Next, ask a student to stand and write his or her name so everyone can see it. Ask that student to answer one or two of the following questions:

- *What do you do at home after school?* (ride a bike, eat dinner, play with friends, finish homework)

- *What do you do on Saturday with your family?* (play ball, laugh, visit family, clean house)

- *What sports, if any, do you play?* (soccer, golf, basketball, football)

- *What do you like to do in your bedroom?* (sleep, watch TV, read, build stuff, listen to music)

Literature Link

The following books are written in terse verse style:
- An Island Grows *by Lola M. Schaefer*
- Pigs Peek *by Rhonda Cox*
- Puffins Climb, Penguins Rhyme *by Bruce McMillan*

- *What do you do with your pet, if you have one?* (race, chase, throw balls, feed it, groom it, shake its paw)

Make sure that whatever you ask will draw a true response. Since we're writing informational text, the responses need to be true statements about the student's behavior.

Write the action word that the student says to the right of his or her name, like this:

	races
Camille	**chases**
	wrestles
	pets

	kicks
Camille	**dribbles**
	passes
	scores

Try to elicit the most specific verbs you can from the student. If she says a boring verb such as *run*, ask, "Which verb describes what you do when you run with the ball down the soccer field?" Your goal is to get the student to come up with language that paints the strongest picture.

After you have brainstormed these verbs together, show the student how to write couplets using the language on display. For instance, a few lines of terse verse for this student might look like the following:

Camille chases.

Camille wrestles.

Camille dribbles.

Camille scores.

All of this is true because Camille really does chase her dog and wrestle with it, and she also dribbles and scores when playing soccer. At this point, have all the students practice writing terse verse. You might say something like this: "I would like each of you to write your name on a piece of paper and think of some specific actions that you do at gymnastics, at football, with your pet, playing an instrument, or with your family. Only write two words, though: Just write your name and a strong action word beside it, please. In a moment, we will share a few of our couplets."

Allow about 5 or 6 minutes for students to write a terse verse about themselves. While they are writing, model writing your own terse verse using the overhead projector or interactive whiteboard.

When students are completing their examples, ask four or five of them to share what they have written later. Celebrate the strongest verbs that you hear.

Writing Terse Verse

When first writing terse verse with your students, select a topic that everyone knows well. This lesson is based on a previous study of vertebrate animals.

Teacher: Let's list five to seven vertebrate animals. Be as specific as you can. For instance, instead of saying "alligators," you can say "American alligators," even though it is two words. Or instead of saying "whales," you might say "orcas" or "right whales" or "humpbacks."

[As students call out animal names, write the words so everyone can see them, leaving generous space between each one.]

Students: Rattlesnakes. Tigers. Bullfrogs. Giraffes. Bald eagles.

Teacher: Great choices! Thank you. As you can see, I've been writing the names of these animals as you've mentioned them. I'd like volunteers to come up and add four verbs beside each animal. But before anyone offers to add a verb, I'd like you to think about the animal. What does it do in the wild? We need to write behaviors that are specific to each animal. All the information we include should be factual.

[Provide a few minutes of quiet for students to think quietly and jot down some notes. Then ask volunteers to come forward and write their choices. A completed prewrite might look like the sample below.]

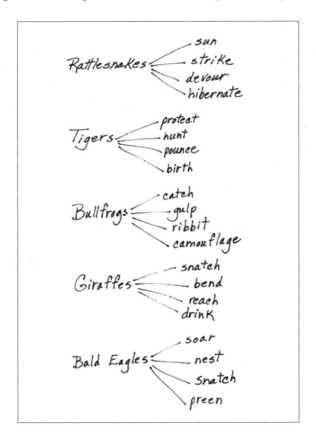

Teacher: Now that our prewrite is complete, I'd like all of you to write a couplet for each animal. For instance, you might write the following:

Giraffes snatch.
Giraffes swallow.

As you can see, I wrote one of the words listed, but I also came up with another active verb on my own—*swallow*. Feel free to use some of the verbs that are listed on our prewrite but also add a few active verbs of your own. Remember, this is informational writing, so each terse verse needs to be factual.

Students' writing will resemble these examples:

- **Tigers crouch.**
- **Tigers pounce.**
- **Giraffes stretch.**
- **Giraffes lick.**
- **Bald eagles soar.**
- **Bald eagles swoop.**

- **Rattlesnakes smell.**
- **Rattlesnakes attack.**
- **Bullfrogs bellow.**
- **Bullfrogs chomp.**

Titles

Titles are optional for terse verse but emphasize to students that a catchy or evocative title is always an extra lure for the reader. You might begin by brainstorming titles for your own topic, pointing out boring titles first, so students will not offer them.

Teacher: Here are some boring titles that I've written. These titles would not lure a reader to my text:

"Animals"

"Vertebrates"

"Vertebrate Animals"

"Animals with an Internal Skeleton"

On the other hand, here are a few catchy titles:

"Backbones on the Move"

"Backbones That Jump and Run"

"Bones and Blood"

"Walking Skeletons"

Some children will probably copy one of your titles, but many will come up with their own. Don't be surprised when they think of titles that are cleverer than yours.

 Nonfiction Writing Lessons That Work © 2012 by Lola M. Schaefer, Scholastic Teaching Resources

As students write, walk behind them and celebrate when you see an original or distinctive action word. This will inspire other students to take a few extra moments to think of other unique verbs. Also, celebrate student writing that is factual. Writing informational or nonfiction text is the ultimate purpose of this structure.

Self-Selected Topics for Terse Verse

Students may select topics for terse verse from their own research or from units in social studies, science, or math. What is important is that they select specific nouns within their topic. For instance, if they have chosen the topic of space, they can brainstorm nouns within that topic, such as *sun, moon, Venus, comets, Earth, black holes*, and so on. Any topic and set of nouns can work, as long as students realize that what they write needs to be factual.

Third-Grade Terse Verse

A student in an ESOL third-grade classroom wrote this terse verse after studying different animal habitats.

Mountain Life

Vultures plunge.

Butterflies flutter.

Owls dive.

Spiders swing.

Coyotes tear.

Rattlesnakes slither.

Deer bounce.

Hawks attack.

Bobcats birth.

As you can see, this student chose not to write in couplets. Encourage students to use a format that best relates the information they know.

The Purpose Behind Writing Terse Verse

Terse verse offers students a concise way to show what they know. Writers have to be specific and know their facts. With a quick read, the audience will be able to tell whether the writer understands the topic well.

Students in a science class developed the following terse verse after studying tectonic plates and the man who first theorized their existence.

Crack! Shift! Drift!

Ortelius studied.

Public misjudged.

Time proved.

Pangea existed.

Magma forced.

Sea floor separated.

Land cracked.

Plates shifted.

Ocean flowed.

Continents began.

Mid-ocean ridge parted.

Evidence appeared.

Scientists concluded.

You can see from what they've written that these students understood exactly what happened throughout time. By grounding their terse verse firmly in the facts, they fulfilled the assignment's essential requirement.

Even if all students don't want to write terse verse now, it is an informational format that they can choose to use in the future.

Process for Independent Writing
Review the steps for writing terse verse with students:
✓ Select a topic.
✓ Brainstorm nouns that are important in that topic. Make a list of four to eight nouns.
✓ Write three or four strong active verbs beside each noun.
✓ Decide which nouns and which verbs you want to use.
✓ Write couplets for each pair of these nouns and verbs.
✓ Give the verse a title if you want.

THE ELEMENTS OF CRAFT

Students practice the following elements of craft while writing terse verse: focus, word choice, organization, subject/verb agreement, and conventions. You can design mini-lessons on any or all of these elements to improve the quality of your students' writing.

Students' Terse Verse

Students wrote the terse verses below after studying geology and seismic activity. Some wrote plain terse verse, and others created their own variation. Feel free to copy these pieces and share them with your own students. The more examples they see, the more comfortable they will be about experimenting with their own ideas.

Caves

On the mushy, green grass . . .

Rain falls.

Water pools.

Ground hollows.

Liquid follows.

Cave forms.

Critters squirm.

Water drips.

Rock rips.

Sound echoes.

Footsteps come closer.

Cave is found,

safe and sound.

by Will Taylor

¡ The Earthquake !

In a city . . .

a building crumbles.

Ground rumbles.

Glass brakes.

Everything shakes.

The city vibrates

DESTRUCTION BEGINS!

Buildings collapse.

Metal chatters.

Plates slide.

People cry.

In another city . . .

a building crumbles.

The ground rumbles.

by Girard Amoyo

continued on next page

Students' Terse Verse, *continued . . .*

Volcanoes

Far, far away at the top of a mountain . . .

A volcano blows.

The lava glows.

Rock shatters.

Lava scatters.

Mountains quake.

People shake.

Another mountain grows.

by Eduardo Magana

Audience/Feedback

Students always appreciate feedback when they write terse verse, whether or not it is published. Many times, they want feedback on their revised drafts. To accomplish this, pair students and have them read their terse verse to one another. Encourage students to read their terse verse aloud twice to ensure that listeners fully comprehend the meaning. A few suggestions for listeners appear below. Select only one suggestion for each set of partners.

- *Listen carefully and then tell the author which couplet painted the strongest images in your mind.*

- *Listen carefully and then tell the author which two verbs—action words—you heard in his or her terse verse.*

- *Listen carefully and then, from the title and the terse verse, tell the author the focus of his or her work.*

CHAPTER 4

Show Information With the Vase Organizer

Our students often learn many different facts about one topic. They might study space and learn interesting information about planets, asteroids, moons, orbits, comets, and black holes. They gain a general understanding of the topic of space, with a few specifics. Or students might study a famous person such as Thomas Edison and learn about his different inventions, his laboratory in Menlo Park, New Jersey, and that he was a mischievous boy who experimented from an early age. In grades 2–5, students usually study a few of the most intriguing or significant facts about topics they learn about in science, math, or social studies.

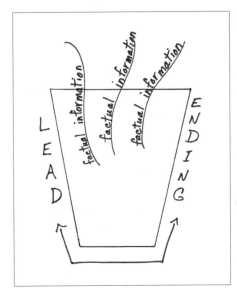

As I mentioned in Chapter 1, many teachers complain that, when they ask students to write what they know, the students simply copy, or plagiarize, facts from different sources. Of course, that's not what we want. We want students engaged in thinking—analyzing, categorizing, comparing, synthesizing.

I've developed a process that enables students to assemble factual information in a cohesive form to show what they know. I call this process the Vase. The Vase begins and ends with general information about a topic, and in the middle, the writer provides individual facts about certain elements or features of that topic.

Exploring the Vase

Materials: *So You Want To Be President* by Judith St. George or a book from the Literature Link on page 34

To begin, read the entire book to your students.

Teacher:	I'm going to go back and read the first page again. Please listen. What factual information did this author write?
Students:	How there are good and bad things about being president; how our presidents live in the White House.
Teacher:	Yes, the author tells us something about all presidents. And it's true. They do live in the White House. Now I'm going to read the last two pages of the book. Please listen carefully. What factual information does the author include in the ending?
Students:	That all presidents take the same oath; that the oath is only 35 words; that all presidents have tried their best, but some have done a better job than others.
Teacher:	Yes. Again, she gives us factual information about all presidents. Now, let's look again at some of the information in the middle of the book. What facts did the author include here?
Students:	Which president was a great swimmer; how many presidents were related; which president had a custom-made bathtub put in the White House; which president put a bowling alley in the White House.
Teacher:	Yes, the middle is filled with information about specific presidents. But the author holds all of those facts together with her lead and ending, which both talk about all the presidents.

Literature Link

The following books include a lead and an ending that focus on a given topic and a middle portion that provides individual facts about certain elements, members, or features of that topic:

- How to Clean a Hippopotamus *by Steve Jenkins & Robin Page*
- An Egg Is Quiet *by Dianna Aston*
- A Seed Is Sleepy *by Dianna Hutts Aston*
- So You Want To Be an Inventor? *by Judith St. George*
- So You Want To Be President? *by Judith St. George*
- Teeth *by Sneed B. Collard III*
- The Train of States *by Peter Sis*
- Unbeatable Beaks *by Stephen Swinburne*

Another good book to use to show this organizational structure is *The Train of States* by Peter Sis. A visual depiction of the Vase appears at the beginning of this title as schoolchildren watch a red, white, and blue locomotive roll past their school windows. The ending shows the students outside the school and a long-distance view of the entire train as it moves out of sight. The middle of the book shows 51 train cars—one for each state and Washington, D.C.—and features state mottos, state birds, the years of statehood, and other relevant facts. The approaching train and the departing train comprise the Vase, while the middle is the individual cars that carry all kinds of information about each of the states and Washington, D.C.

Writing the Vase

Materials: an interactive whiteboard, overhead projector, or chart paper

Model the following process so students can see each of its steps.

Teacher: Let's explore this informational structure called the Vase. We will make a prewrite for the Vase. You can copy it in your writer's notebook or on a separate piece of paper. Since we just completed a study of Native American life, let's use that as our model.

[*First draw the outline of the Vase.*]

Now we want our lead and our ending to connect in some way. We could have a lead that mentions something that all Native Americans believed or did. We could have a lead that starts the day in an Indian village. We might even have a lead that describes the setting of an Indian village.

[*Ask one student to make a choice.*]

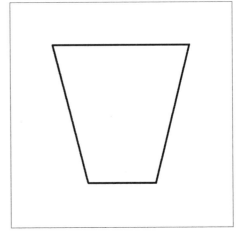

Teacher: What kind of lead do you want to select for our informational writing on Native Americans?

Omar: The start of the day.

Teacher: What would a young Native American see or hear or do first thing in the morning? What could our lead be?

Omar: As the sun rises, the smell of campfire fills our village.

Teacher: Wow! What a perfect lead. Thank you. I'm going to write a few reminder words of this lead on the left side of the vase. I will write "sun rises— smell of campfire."

Now we need an ending that will connect to the lead. What could a young Native American see, hear, or do at the end of the day?

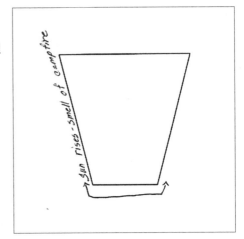

Omar: As the sun sets, the songs of our people fill the night air.

Teacher: Wow again! That's a perfect connection to the lead. I'll go ahead and write these reminder words on the right side of the Vase: "sun sets— songs of people."

Now we need to decide what kind of information about Native Americans we would want to develop in the middle of our writing. Any suggestions? What facts would you like to include?

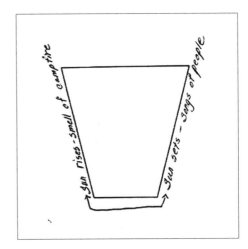

Trevor: We could talk about their different kinds of homes.

Sachi: Or the tools that they used.

Barack: About how they got their food.

Teacher: These would make excellent facts to include in the middle. Let me draw three stems in our Vase. The stems will remind us of the detailed facts we want to write about in the middle of our informational piece.

Now I'm going to write a few reminder words on each stem. After the word "homes," what should I write?

Students: Teepees, longhouses, wigwams, lodges, hogans, pueblos.

Teacher: Thank you. I will add those words. And after the word "tools," what should I write?

Students: Ax, mallet, needle, arrowhead, basket.

Teacher: I will add those, as well. Thank you. I've written the word "food." What would you like me to add?

Students: Corn, beans, and squash, fish, wild animals.

Teacher: I have added these to another stem. Here is our completed prewrite.

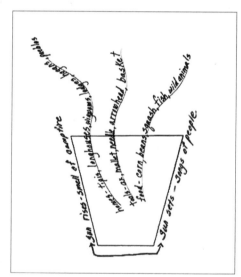

[*Once you have completed a prewrite with your students, the writing of the Vase goes quickly.*]

Using the ideas in the reminder words on the left of the Vase, craft a lead of one or two sentences that can begin your writing. Remember, this is informational writing, so your lead should be factual.

[*Provide time for students to write their leads. Have three or four students share their lead and encourage celebrations of what they did well.*]

Select one of the stems in the middle of the Vase. Each stem holds specific words that will remind you of specific details of the daily life of Native Americans. Write two or three sentences that will provide your reader with factual information.

[*Repeat this process for one or two more stems.*]

When you have completed your factual details, it is time to craft an ending. Read the reminder words on the right side of the vase. Write an ending with one or two sentences that will connect to the lead.

As with all writing, length is not as important as how well-written and focused the writing is. Second and third graders might only develop a lead, two middle sections, and an ending. That's great. Fourth and fifth graders need to be able to decide if they want to develop two, three, or four middle sections for their writing.

Self-Selected Topics for the Vase

Quite a few science and social studies topics lend themselves to the Vase. I've seen students use this structure to write about plants, rocks and minerals, space, simple machines, energy, Greek civilization, branches of the U.S. government, topographic regions of a state, habitats, vertebrates, and weather.

Student Vase Writing

Garett planned and wrote the following report about the *Hindenburg* after reading a piece of nonfiction on this topic in reading class.

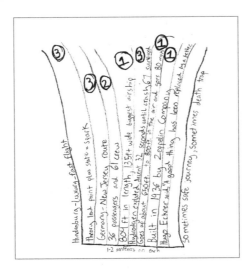

The *Hindenburg* by Garett McVay

The 1936 *Hindenburg* was the new marvelous way to fly, the biggest airship and the most luxurious. It was a fine piece of machinery and offered fast flight over the blue depths of the Atlantic Ocean.

This jaw-dropping air machine was built by the Zeppelin Company. It was eight hundred, four feet long and one hundred, thirty five feet wide. That's huge! The *Hindenburg* flew between six hundred fifty feet and eight hundred feet in the air and around

continued on next page

Student Vase Writing, *continued . . .*

eighty miles per hour. That's fast for something that big!

On the day of its flight, thirty-six passengers and sixty-one workers boarded for a total of ninety-seven. That's around two people waiting on one person! Only the rich got to go on that airship.

It cruised up into the air above Germany on its way to New Jersey. The take-off was so smooth that you wouldn't know you were in the air unless you were looking out the window! After around two and a half days, the *Hindenburg* arrived after being held back by a thunderstorm. As the *Hindenburg* was landing, there was a sudden explosion. In thirty-two seconds, the airship was on the ground in a pile of steel and ash. Sixty-seven people survived the crash. Some people believe that it was the static electricity in the air or the lead in the paint that caused the spark to explode the hydrogen. Others believe it was a bomb. No matter which way, it was a terrible explosion. Another tragedy in the era of invention.

Sometimes a luxurious and safe flight, but after the *Hindenburg*, these airships were known as deathtraps. The Zeppelins lost all their fame. Later airplanes came, and the inventor of Zeppelins, Hugo Eckener, said, "A good thing has been replaced by a better."

Titanic by Kristina Chapple

"The ship of dreams" the survivors called it. This is also known as the *Titanic*, one of the greatest ships of all time. Not only was its wreckage devastating, but also the loss of many lives.

From 1909 to 1912, 3,000 people helped build this "hotel on water." Then on April 10, 1912, it was ready to set sail. This was not only a grand ship, it was also very prodigious. It had many compartments, but very few lifeboats!

Then on April 14, 1912, just four days out on her maiden voyage, the *Titanic* struck an iceberg on her starboard side. In just two hours and ten minutes the ocean water had flooded six into the seventh compartment. The unsinkable ship was doomed!

The *Titanic* only had 1.5-2 hours left afloat. These last moments were full of chaos. The crew had to hand out all the life jackets. The radio operator sent off many distress calls, but most of the other ships were fast asleep. The *Titanic* also turned on search

continued on next page

continued . . .

lights. A ship ten miles away, the *Californian*, saw them, but didn't respond.

Then, a glimmer of hope. *Carpathia*, the Titanic's sister ship heard a distress call. Although she was 58 miles away, the boat turned around and headed for the sinking ship. *Carpathia* arrived at 4:10 A.M., one hour and fifty minutes after the wreck. This ship saved 706 people, but with 2,223 passengers on board, it was still very tragic.

The *Titanic* might well be one of the biggest disasters of time. In my mind, the *Titanic* will always be one of the most magical, beautiful, despairing and fascinating ships ever to be.

If your students use a writer's notebook, encourage them to record possible topics near the Vase prewrite graphic. This should be an ongoing process throughout the year. As students study pioneer life, they might make notes about some of the hazards that pioneers encountered while moving West. If they are studying Colonial America, they might add the topics of famous statesmen or some of the many conflicts with the British.

One fifth-grade girl chose to use the Vase to write about vascular plants for science class. She began her piece with this lead:

Fingers reach into a paper packet. Seeds lie side by side in the warm earth. Trowels carve deep holes. Bulbs, the size of fists, are nestled in the soil. Hands plunge roots into the moist ground.

Her ending read:

After the plants mature, sunflowers blossom making more seeds. Lilies open showing their summer color. And ferns spread their fronds up and over the garden.

In the middle, this student wrote about the different parts of the plant, from roots to stem, leaves to flowers. She gave specific information about the roles of these parts.

The Purpose Behind the Vase

The Vase provides students with a structure that lets them share lots of interesting facts that they learn about a topic. These facts do not have to be in any chronological or prioritized order. But the Vase does require higher-order thinking, because students have to select a lead and an ending that are both factual and connected. As with riddles, poems, sidebars, terse verse, and several other structures described in this book, the Vase writing can be planned and written in one or two days. The result is that the student feels satisfaction, and the teacher can easily see what that student knows about the topic.

Process for Independent Writing

Review the steps for completing a Vase prewrite with students:

✓ Select a topic you know well. Take a few moments to decide on a lead that is factual and general. Jot a couple of reminder words to yourself on the left side of the vase.

✓ Now craft an ending that ties to your lead. Again, it needs to be factual and general. Jot a couple of reminder words on the right side of the vase.

✓ Draw three or four stems in the vase and decide which specific features, elements, events, people, accomplishments, or jobs you want to detail. Write three to five reminder words on each stem.

✓ When the prewrite is complete, write a lead and continue to write the rest of your informational piece. Remember to take your time and write two or three sentences for each of your middle facts.

THE ELEMENTS OF CRAFT

Students practice the following elements of craft while writing informational Vase pieces: focus, word choice, details and development, organization, fluency, voice, and conventions. You can design mini-lessons on any or all of these elements to improve the quality of student writing.

Audience/Feedback

Materials: paper or sticky notes

Every student wants to receive feedback on his or her writing. With the Vase, I suggest that students either post their drafts in the hall or read them to a small group of classmates. If students post their writing in the hall, they will need to pose a question to their readers, so provide paper or sticky notes for written responses. The questions offer readers a purpose for returning to the writing and reading it again. A few suggestions for the question are listed below.

- *Which fact interested you the most?*
- *Read my lead and my ending. How do they connect?*
- *How many different facts did you read in this piece of writing?*

If a student chooses to read the informational piece to classmates rather than post it in the hall, here are some questions that he or she might pose to elicit responses. One or two questions, such as the following, will suffice:

- *Since this is informational writing, what facts did you hear?*
- *Which fact was the most interesting to you?*
- *Did my lead and ending connect? How?*

CHAPTER 5

Show What You Know Through Poetry

Poetry is one text structure that frightens some teachers. Maybe it's because these teachers never wrote poetry while they were in school, or maybe it's because poetry can take so many different forms. Thankfully, though, students embrace poetry. They enjoy its economy of words and emphasis on meaning and word choice. They know that in poetry, punctuation is not as important as the focus and development of one image or idea.

Exploring Informational Poetry

Materials: collections of informational and nonfiction poetry (see the Literature Link on page 43)

Begin by reading several informational and nonfiction poems to students. It's better if you also display the poems so everyone can see them as you read. I tend to read a poem at least two times, usually more. On the first reading, students will think about the general meaning and the focus of the poem. On the second or third readings, it is easier for them to visualize images and take note of the structure of the poem.

   After each poem, ask two or three questions, such as the ones in the model lesson below. For this demonstration model, I'm using the poem "If I Were the Equator" by Kathryn Madeline Allen (from *Got Geography!* by Lee Bennett Hopkins).

Teacher: What's the focus of this poem? In other words, what is the big idea that the poet is writing about?

Students: She's pretending to be the equator. She's saying what she would do if she were the equator.

Teacher: Do you hear, or do you see, any factual information in this poem? What is it?

[It's always a good idea to reread the poem and stop after every three or four lines so students can remember the facts that they hear.]

Students: No degrees latitude; other lines running east to west; 25,000 miles; equal distance from the poles; splits the globe in half; between the tropics.

Teacher: Wow! You're listening well today. Do you hear any terms or words that are specific to the topic? I'll read the poem again and stop every so often.

Students: *Latitude*; *east and west*; *miles*; *poles*; *tropics.*

Teacher: Fantastic! What is your favorite line in the poem? Why do you like that line? I'll read the poem one more time and then you can tell me.

Students: "I would have an attitude"; "with nearly 25,000 miles I clearly am the best"; "makes me the one—the only one— who splits the globe in half."

Teacher: What you mentioned are the poetic parts that the poet weaves in between her facts. Poetry is looking at the ordinary in an extraordinary kind of way. If the poet had just listed fact after fact, it really wouldn't be a poem. Instead, she decided to put herself in the role of the equator. She mixed human qualities with real information about the equator. That's why this poem works so well.

𝓛iterature 𝓛ink

Here are a few poetry books that include informational or nonfiction poems for students in grades 2–5.

- Earthshake
  by Lisa Westberg Peters
- Got Geography! *selected by Lee Bennett Hopkins*
- in the swim
  by Douglas Florian
- Lives: Poems About Famous Americans *selected by Lee Bennett Hopkins*
- Spectacular Science *selected by Lee Bennett Hopkins*
- When Clay Sings
  by Byrd Baylor

Writing Informational Poetry

Materials: several informational or nonfiction poems, chart paper and marker or an interactive whiteboard

Read several poems that are about real things in the real world. When your students get anxious to write, plan and draft a poem together.

Ask students to sit near you. Use chart paper or an interactive whiteboard to record and display the different stages of the poem's development.

Teacher: Informational or nonfiction poetry is all about focus, images, and facts mixed with a poetic element that makes it original. Let's start with focus. Lately we have been studying simple machines in science. Let's focus on one of those machines and write a poem about it. Which simple machine would you like to write a poem about?

Students: Wheel and axle; inclined plane; pulley; lever; wedge.

Teacher: Let's select the one that everyone knows the most about. Spencer, which simple machine should be our focus?

Spencer: The wheel and axle.

Teacher: I'm writing the words "Wheel and Axle" at the top of the right side of the board. Since this is informational writing, we need some facts about the wheel and axle. What do we know?

Students: The wheel's round. It's a simple machine. The wheel can roll or turn. Sometimes it can hold or lift things. It makes work easier. The axle is fixed. The bigger the wheel, the greater the force. It's used in other machines.

[As students respond, record key words on the right side of the chart or board.]

Teacher: As you can see, I have been writing down a few reminder words for the different facts that you have listed. Now, let's list just action words that have something to do with a wheel.

Students: *Roll; move; carry; transport; turn; lift; raise; twist.*

Teacher: Great list! Thank you. Besides action words, what other words can we add that you think of when you think of "wheel and axle"?

Students: *Round; circle; steering wheel; easier; less work; mechanical.*

Teacher: Now, let's reread "If I Were the Equator" one more time so we can look at the line breaks. Poets decide which words they want to put on a line, and the line is usually not a complete sentence. They do want at least one important word on a line, though. Sometimes poets break a line for dramatic effect. Look at how Kathryn Allen does that with the line "makes me the one—the only one—who." Right away, you want to know what it makes her the only one to do.

The poet doesn't complete that thought right away. She leaves a white space— a break in the lines. White space gives pause. It lets the reader think for a moment or anticipate what might happen next. You, too, can create a poem with white space. But don't overdo it. Use white space sparingly to make a point or to get your reader's attention.

Wheel and Axle

round

simple machine

roll or turn

hold or lift

makes work easier

fixed axle

bigger wheel, greater force

in machines

roll, move, carry, transport, turn, lift,

raise, twist

round, circle, steering wheel,

easier, less work, mechanical

Teacher:	Poems look like poems. They don't look like paragraphs. Each line needs to add something important to the total poem.
	Let's start our poem. Do you want to be the voice of the wheel and axle, or do you want to write a poem about the wheel and axle?
Lucas:	Let's write a poem about it.
Teacher:	OK. The great thing about poetry is that you just start with an image. Let's look at our list of facts. Which one should be our starting image? What do you want to say first about a wheel and axle for your audience?
Spencer:	Let's start with what it is—a simple machine.
Teacher:	Now, if we were writing an explanatory paragraph, we would write, "A wheel and axle is a simple machine." But this is a poem. We want images that are appealing to our audience. How do you want to write this information?
May:	It's simple. A simple machine.
Teacher:	Great. That has a lot of energy. Let me add that on the left side of our board. Now, what do simple machines do?
Max:	They work. They make work easier.
Teacher:	We need our next line, or group of lines, to be about the work that a wheel and axle does.
Finn:	Work. Work. Work. I like how poets sometimes repeat a word.
Teacher:	That's great. Let me add that. Do you want all of those words on the same line, or do you want me to stagger them down the page, or have one word above the other two? These are some of the choices that poets can make.
Omar:	Let's put them going up—you know, like how a wheel and axle can sometimes lift something.
Teacher:	Excellent! Let me try that. So far our poem is exciting. It's going to grab a reader's attention. Now, what does a wheel and axle do for work?
Trevor:	It makes work easy.
Jasmine:	It's less work.
Max:	It takes less force.
Teacher:	What would you like me to write about that?
Keisha:	Make it easy. With little force.
Teacher:	Great. Let me add that. Now, we need some of those action words that you brainstormed to show what a wheel and axle do when it's working.
Spencer:	Twisting. Turning.
May:	Yes, but since it's a simple machine, we don't sweat. Can we add, "without sweat" after "twisting, turning"?
Teacher:	Absolutely. Let me write down both of those lines.

Teacher: This poem is really shaping up. Now we need to tell the audience what we're talking about and have a grand slam ending—something poetic.

Cyd: Wheel and axle work together.

Ellie: To make your life simple. Only, can we do some of that white space before the word *simple*?

Teacher: Yes. Let me go ahead and write that much. Let's read what we have so far. It's looking good. Now we need an ending. Maybe it can repeat something you said earlier.

Spencer: Simple machine. It tells the reader what it's all about again.

Teacher: Nice touch. Repetition in a poem is always good. Let me write that. Now, let's look back at the facts or the terms that you brainstormed. Is there perhaps one more term that you would like to add to the poem? We don't need a separate line. I think your ending works well the way you have it. But we could add a term or fact to the poem if you want.

Roberto: *Mechanical*—that's a good term and we could add it to our poem.

Teacher: Ooooh, *mechanical* would add a good science term. Where would you like to add that?

Roberto: Right after "sweat." We could kind of repeat the beginning by saying, "It's mechanical. A mechanical wonder."

	Wheel and Axle

Teacher: You are all using such specific words. That's why this poem is so meaningful. Let me add that. OK, let's read your poem together out loud.

Teacher: What science terms do you see and hear?

Students: *Mechanical*; *work*; *machine*; *simple machine*; *force*; *wheel and axle*.

Teacher: What facts do you see and hear? What is something that a wheel and axle does?

Students: It turns. It twists. It makes work easy.

Teacher: I think you've written a masterful poem. Congratulations.

Wheel and Axle

It's simple.
A simple machine.
                    Work.
        Work.
Work.
Make it easy
with little force.
Twisting, turning,
without sweat.
It's mechanical.
A mechanical wonder.
Wheel and axle
work together
to make your life . . .
simple.
Simple machine.

 Nonfiction Writing Lessons That Work © 2012 by Lola M. Schaefer, Scholastic Teaching Resources

Make sure you hang each collaborative poem with the prewrite that accompanied it. This gives students a working model when they are ready to write their own informational or nonfiction poems.

Self-Selected Topics for Poetry

You will be surprised by the number of topics that lend themselves to writing informational or nonfiction poetry. Published poetry collections and anthologies show that no topic—from earthquakes to Thomas Edison to flounder to Amelia Earhart—is unavailable to the poet who wants to show what he or she knows. If students have their own writer's notebook, have them include a section where they can record all the topics that they know well. They might select some of these topics for writing poetry, others for writing an informational story, or still others for writing sidebars or compare-and-contrast reports. The reading of well-chosen poems is the best way to teach your students about form, word choice, style, and information. Use these poems to ignite a fire in your students and give them permission to select their own topics.

The Purpose Behind Writing Poetry

Poetry is a writing structure that offers immense freedom. Students can think about their topics and decide on the kind of poem they want to write. Poetry enables students to focus on the importance of their topic, select terms that match their topic, and create images that are accessible to the audience.

Here are two student samples:

Fort Sumter

Boom!
The cannons went off
no sleep for the soldiers
the smell of death
and not any food
the battle
long battles
and the little men.

For Adrian, reading about what happened at Fort Sumter made the impression that war takes away our basic comforts. His poem shows that he thinks that fighting and battles are enormous and they make humans feel little.

Lanier wrote this poem about slavery before and during the Civil War era.

What is freedom?

Blacks were suffering

from lack of food

But they still asked themselves

What is freedom?

They kept struggling to be free.

Some fought back

but they all lost

They still asked

What is freedom?

Still no respect.

Lanier shows us with his words how great he felt the struggle for freedom was at this time. The slaves had so little to begin with, but they struggled. They had a goal: to find out what freedom would be like.

Process for Independent Writing

Review the steps for writing informational or nonfiction poetry with students:

- ✓ Select a topic for an informational poem.

- ✓ Brainstorm reminder words on the topic. Include any important terms, names, dates, and events. Add active verbs if they are pertinent to the topic. Make sure that all your notes are factual.

- ✓ Look over your list of reminder words and use the words to select an image to begin the poem. Add three to five more images. Again, make sure the information is factual. Write the images in poetic form rather than in paragraphs.

- ✓ Make use of line breaks and white space.

- ✓ Add a poetic device such as alliteration, personification, metaphor, simile, repeating refrain, or unique point of view.

- ✓ Reread the poem. Check that there are at least three facts. Eliminate any images that are off-topic or are not factual.

- ✓ Give the poem a title if you want.

 Nonfiction Writing Lessons That Work © 2012 by Lola M. Schaefer, Scholastic Teaching Resources

THE ELEMENTS OF CRAFT

Students practice the following elements of craft when writing informational poetry: focus, word choice, tone, voice, and figurative language. You can design mini-lessons on any or all of these elements to improve the quality of student writing.

Third-Grade Informational Poetry

Students created this poem after a study of rocks and minerals and the forces that form them. Look for facts!

Minerals, Just Minerals

A volcano erupts and rock hardens
diamonds glimmer in a mountain cave
as moonlight shines above
layers and layers join together
becoming rocks at last
heat and pressure
make spots and bruises
on me
even though I keep on changing
I still love myself—metamorphic rock
rocks are minerals, just minerals.

by Alexandra Reid

continued on next page

Igneous, Here I Come

Deep under ground
  bubbling
    hot and steamy
      thick, chunky
        waiting to burst out
          waiting to cool down
            waiting to become a rock
              black and red hot lava
                steaming down
                  Here I come!
                    I rush down to cool
                      to become a rock
                        a volcano once quiet
                          then active
                            rumbled
                              like a sign
                                that the tank was full
                                  then it shot me out
                                    like a cannon
                                      I went high, then low
                                        I cooled and became a rock
                                          igneous, here I come

by Nadira Javid

And here is the poem that the teacher wrote while her students created their poetry.

Igneous Obnoxious

Kasplat!!
  Akchooo!!
    Blooogh!!
I spew volcanic molten lava all over you!
Ha Ha

continued on next page

continued . . .

It's hot, so hot you
can't stand it
As I ooze on down
your lovely planet
Slowly I creep
   cooling along my way
    forming BLACK POROUS PUMICE
Ahem! Allow me to scrub the
    dead skin off your feet
for Igneous Obnoxious can
never be sweet!

How About A Title?

It is up to the student whether or not to give a poem a title. Some poems have titles, some do not, but a title needs to set the tone of the poem and give the reader a hint of the topic. For instance, the collaborative poem about a wheel and axle in the Writing Informational Poetry section could also be titled "No Sweat." A poem about the life cycle of a butterfly could be called "Hatch. Eat. Fly." Or a poem about subtraction could be called "Take It Away!" Post a few published poems that have titles in the classroom and some that do not. This support will help students as they write their own poems and make decisions about a title.

Audience/Feedback

Materials: an interactive whiteboard, large sheets of paper and markers

Since part of writing poetry is the actual look of it on the page, I suggest you find ways to display your students' informational poetry so the audience can see the poems as well as read or hear them. For instance, you might scan some of the poems into your computer and display them on the interactive whiteboard. Or you might have students copy their poems onto a large sheet of paper so you can put them on display in the hall. With any display method you use, ask the audience to respond to one or two of the questions below. You might also have students copy their poems to the whiteboard in your classroom and, again, the audience could write comments in response to one or two of the questions below.

- *Which image in this poem paints the strongest picture in your mind?*
- *Since poetry looks at the ordinary in an extraordinary way, which line or image in this poem makes you think differently about the topic?*
- *How many facts can you find in this poem?*
- *How many terms can you find in this poem?*
- *What are the two strongest verbs in this poem?*
- *When did you first know* what the topic of this poem was?

Nonfiction Writing Lessons That Work © 2012 by Lola M. Schaefer, Scholastic Teaching Resources

CHAPTER 6

Show Differences With Compare and Contrast

This chapter will offer suggestions on how to help your students use the compare-and-contrast structure in their informational or nonfiction writing. This structure can provide support to our students when we ask them to think more deeply about their social studies, science, or math units. From my experience, I know that this form of writing engages students in meaningful conversations and provides immense satisfaction when they complete it.

Noting similarities and differences among animals in a habitat, historical events, the many forms of energy, or the number operations requires both knowledge and thought. Whenever we ask students to compare and contrast, they will read their resources again, study specific features, and make decisions about which information is important and what isn't.

Exploring Compare and Contrast

Materials: *Now & Ben* by Gene Baretta or a book with a strong compare-and-contrast structure (see Literature Link on page 54)

Begin by reading a few pages from the book. *Now & Ben*, which is used in the model lessons in this chapter, shows the contrast between an invention that Ben Franklin created and how it appears and is used today. Ask your students a few of the following questions about the text, depending on which invention you are viewing:

- Why did Ben create this invention? Why do we use it today?

- What are the differences between how it was used then and how it is used today?

- Study the invention now and then. What materials were used in Ben's invention? What materials are used in today's application?

- Do you use any of these inventions today? Why or why not?

Writing Compare and Contrast

Materials: *Now & Ben* or a similar book (see Literature Link); chart paper, an interactive whiteboard, or overhead projector, paper and pencils

Literature Link

Both of these books will help students think about historical events in a compare/contrast framework:

- Neo Leo *by Gene Barretta*
- Now & Ben *by Gene Barretta*

To begin this writing lesson, ask students to consider the title of *Now & Ben*. Refer again to a few pages in the book and note how the word *now* is used to introduce what we do today and how the name *Ben* is used to introduce what the inventor did long ago.

Draw a T-chart on chart paper, an interactive whiteboard, or an overhead projector so the entire class can view it. Then ask two students to come forward. Write each student's name at the top of a column.

Teacher: I'm going to ask you a few questions about you and your families. We will display your different answers in this two-column planning sheet. Here's the first question: *Do you have any pets? If so, what are they?*

[*Record students' responses under the proper headings. Continue this process for the rest of the answers.*]

Teacher: *How many brothers and sisters do you have?*
What is the first thing that you usually do on Saturday mornings after breakfast?
What is your favorite meal?
Describe a family activity that you all enjoy.

Your completed graphic might look something like this:

José	Maddie
dog: Sparky	cat: Leo, bird: Aretha
2 brothers, 4 sisters	5 sisters, 0 brothers
Sat: play/Sparky, ride bike	Sat: read/bed, draw
hamburger/potato salad/green beans	spaghetti/meatballs/garlic toast
fam: Frisbee golf, making cookies	fam: roller-skating, movies

Teacher: Just like the author of the book *Now & Ben*, we need to think about how to introduce the information about José and Maddie. We could say, "In José's home . . ." and "In Maddie's home . . ." and then write our information about these two students. What are some other choices?

Students: José told us that he . . .	Maddie told us that she . . .
In José's world . . .	In Maddie's world . . .
The truth about José is . . .	The truth about Maddie is . . .

After one student selects an introductory phrase for the information from both students (the phrases don't have to be the same), you are ready to guide everyone in writing. For this structure, I always suggest that students fold a sheet of paper in half lengthwise. This naturally makes two columns. At the top of one column, they write an introductory phrase for José, and at the top of the other column they write an introductory phrase for Maddie.

Since this is just practice, I ask students to write two different points to compare and contrast between the students.

Teacher: Now, we take these reminder words and turn them into complete thoughts with details. For instance, for José I might write the following:

The truth about José is . . .
that he enjoys grilled hamburgers, his mom's homemade potato salad, and a big pile of fresh green beans for dinner.

And for Maddie I might write the following:

The truth about Maddie is . . .
that her favorite meal is spaghetti and meatballs covered in cheese, with garlic toast right out of the oven.

Students do not need to rewrite their introductory phrases each time. They can write the phrases at the top of the page with an ellipsis so they can simply complete the sentence with their facts about each student. A completed practice piece might look like this:

The truth about José is . . .	**The truth about Maddie is . . .**
he enjoys grilled hamburgers, homemade potato salad, and fresh green beans.	she looks forward to a dinner of spaghetti and meatballs and garlic toast right out of the oven.
that on Saturday mornings, he likes to play tug-of-war with his dog Sparky and ride his bike around the neighborhood.	she likes to go back to bed on Saturday mornings and curl up with a good book. Later she gets out her markers and draws.
he likes to play Frisbee golf with his family. On rainy days, they make raisin-oatmeal cookies.	that nothing makes her happier than a day spent skating at the roller rink and an evening at the movies.

Self-Selected Topics for Compare-and-Contrast Writing

After collaborative writing, students are always eager to write their own compare-and-contrast pieces. The choice of topics is wide open, but as with all writing, you want to show that the more focused the topic is, the better. One strategy that provides support to students in grades 2–5 is to brainstorm familiar topics that would work well for this writing structure.

All state standards include studies of famous people, as these examples show:

- **Wisconsin Grade 4 Social Studies standard B.4.7:** Identify and describe important events and famous people in Wisconsin and United States history.

- **Montana Grade 4 Social Studies 4.4:** Students will identify and describe famous people, important democratic values (e.g., democracy, freedom, justice), symbols (e.g., Montana and U.S. flags, state flower), and holidays, in the history of Montana, American Indian tribes, and the United States.

To meet these standards, students could compare and contrast transportation, communication, clothing, and business between the lifetimes of two different famous people—whether they are American leaders, explorers, or inventors. Or students might choose to compare the daily life of a famous person to their own daily lives. I've seen students respond energetically to the task of comparing four or five features of a single time period, such as pioneer life in the 1800s, with their own lives.

Once when I was working with a primary class, the teacher asked students to write about Harriet Tubman. I offered children a choice of several different text structures, and they chose compare and contrast. They compared Harriet Tubman's daily life—no shoes, enslavement, finding food on the road, leading people on the Underground Railroad—to their own lives. Students worked collaboratively to list about six items in daily life on both sides. Then each student chose three features to compare and contrast. Some students copied ideas listed on the interactive whiteboard, and other students came up with their own features of daily life to compare. In this particular case, students didn't have choice of topic, but they did have choice of structure and content. Try to encourage all these elements with your students—the more personal choice they have, the greater their commitment to writing will be.

In social studies, students might want to compare:

- two specific state regions or habitats
- two battles in the same war
- weapons used in two different conflicts
- a monarchy and a democracy
- the role of coastal cities and those that are inland
- the formation of two different landforms

In science, students might want to compare:

- the hunting and eating habits of two different animals

 Nonfiction Writing Lessons That Work © 2012 by Lola M. Schaefer, Scholastic Teaching Resources

- adaptations of two different plants that live in the same ecosystem
- the availability and use of one fossil fuel with another
- the efficiency of one fossil fuel and one alternative energy source
- the nutrients found in two different vegetables, or one vegetable and one fruit
- atomic fusion and atomic fission

In math, students might want to compare:

- one geometric shape to another
- the purpose and use of one computational process to another
- prime and composite numbers
- one problem-solving technique to another
- the commutative property and the associative property

It often helps students to list these kinds of writing ideas in a writer's notebook. As compare-and-contrast topics are mentioned, students can record them for a future writing project.

The Purpose Behind Compare and Contrast

Compare and contrast is designed to push students into analysis—into thinking about the different features or elements of a topic and the relationships between them. This is higher-order thinking at its best. It's also pure informational writing. Understanding relationships—the interdependence, impact, or connections—between groups of people, animals, planets, machines, forms of energy, or any content is at the core of what we want for our students.

In this type of structure, the writer does not get sidetracked by thinking about leads or paragraphs or endings. This structure is straightforward, allowing students to think strictly about content and analyze the facts before them.

Automatic Differentiation

I usually request that students compare and contrast three or four elements or features of their two topics. However, I never require everyone to write about a certain number of them. That way, students who need differentiation can write more or less. If you have students in your classroom who still struggle to write their ideas in a meaningful way, allow them to compare and contrast two elements or features. It's students' thinking that is important in informational writing, not the length.

Process for Independent Writing

Review the steps for using the compare-and-contrast structure:

✓ Select two topics or time periods to compare and contrast.

✓ Create a two-column planning sheet. Write each topic at the top of a different column.

✓ Compare or contrast the same feature, event, element, or trait for each topic. Use only a few reminder words and phrases rather than complete sentences. Remember, the information has to be factual.

✓ Write an introductory phrase for each topic. These phrases will set the tone for the writing. Use an ellipsis (. . .) at the end of each phrase.

✓ Select one of the features, events, elements, or traits from your planning sheet and write a factual statement about that information. Include at least one detail.

✓ Repeat this process for the other topic, and then continue comparing and contrasting the other points.

✓ Give your writing a title if you want.

 ### THE ELEMENTS OF CRAFT

Students practice the following elements of craft while writing compare and contrast: focus, organization, tone, word choice (terms), voice, the use of an ellipsis, and conventions. You can design mini-lessons on any or all of these elements to improve the quality of student writing.

Supports for Compare and Contrast

The more visual samples you offer your students while they are writing, the more successful they will be in their independent practice. You might post a list of introductory phrases in the classroom where everyone can see them. The list is not posted so students copy from it, but rather to show them the variety and possibilities as they brainstorm on their own. Here are some examples:

Under the harvest moon . . .	**Between the highways . . .**
In Thomas Edison's laboratory . . .	**On the Calypso with Jacques Cousteau . . .**
In the canopy of the rainforest . . .	**In the reeds of the marsh . . .**
When dividing . . .	**While multiplying . . .**
When the sun is overhead . . .	**When constellations fill the skies . . .**

It is also helpful to have a written sample of a two-column compare-and-contrast planning sheet available so students can use it as a guide during independent practice.

Under the harvest moon . . .	**In a solar-powered home . . .**
ancient Pueblo Indians cooked their dinner over open pits while sharing their stories of the day.	a family cooks its dinner on an electric stove, then sits on chairs around a table, sharing the day's events.
the Pueblo Indians gathered water to drink and clean with from channels that they chiseled in the stone canyon where they lived.	parents and children turn on faucets to get drinking water or run showers or baths. Both warm and cold water flow through pipes from a water source that could be a well or a city water tower.
ancient Pueblos made clothing from local plants and the hides and fur of animals. Usually, each person had one pair of moccasins that were worn until they fell apart.	family members open their closets and select factory-made clothing. Some is made from plants such as cotton and the wool of sheep or the hides of animals, but most clothing is made from human-made materials. And almost everyone has several pairs of shoes for sports, work, and play.

Audience/Feedback

Students enjoy reading their compare-and-contrast writing with a partner. To do this, you will need to make a copy of one student's work and give that copy to the other student. Then have the two students stand on opposite sides of the room. The writer reads the introductory phrase on the left side and then the first fact listed under it. The partner then reads the introductory phrase on the right side and the first fact listed under it. They take turns reading the information in each column. Having two voices offers a contrast and makes the listening experience more interesting for the audience. At the end of the reading, have the audience supply feedback. Some suggestions appear below; ask the audience to answer only one or two of these questions. The writer can even tell the audience before the reading what kind of feedback he or she would appreciate.

- *Which introductory phrase did you appreciate the most? Why?*
- *What two facts did you hear that you felt were the most specific?*
- *What were the two most interesting facts that you heard in this writing?*
- *What was the greatest contrast between the two topics?*
- *What terms—words specific to the topics—did you hear in the writing? Name two or three terms.*

Nonfiction Writing Lessons That Work © 2012 by Lola M. Schaefer, Scholastic Teaching Resources

CHAPTER 7

Show Information in Story

Story is as old as civilization. First oral tellings, then pictographs, and, eventually, the written word were shared to convey the emotions and events of humans. Story connects person to person, no matter how different the culture or great the distance. Not surprisingly, many children, especially those who are strong readers, like to show what they know through story.

Exploring Informational Story

Materials: informational or nonfiction picture books (see Literature Link on page 63)

To begin a discussion of story, I have students raise a fist in front of their face. "This is a story character," I say. "Every good story has a believable, likable character." Then I ask them to raise their other hand, fingers together, palm facing the fist. "This is either a job the character needs to complete, or it is a problem that the character must solve."

   Then I bang my fist lightly against my open palm. "Plot, or conflict, is made up of the events or the attempts of the character to complete the job or solve the problem. Your character will always make at least three different efforts to solve the problem or complete the job." Now

Story character

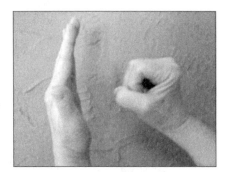

The character needs to complete a job or solve a problem.

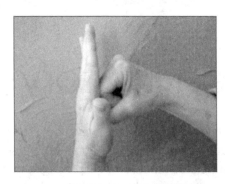

The character tries to complete the job or solve the problem (plot).

The character completes the job or solves the problem (resolution).

my fist opens, and the fingers of that hand cover the fingertips of my other hand. "When the character finally resolves the problem or completes the job, the story ends."

Then I read a picture book to the class that either offers scientific information within the story or a historical setting (see the Literature Link on the next page).

After reading the book, I ask the following questions:

- *Who was the main character in this book?*
- *What job or problem created the conflict or struggle for the character?*
- *Did you hear any scientific terms in this story?*
- *Did you hear any references to famous people or historical events or periods?*

Before having students attempt to write informational stories, I repeat the above process with a different book two or three more times. It is important for children to think about story elements and see how other writers add the informational layer.

Writing Informational Story

Materials: an interactive whiteboard, a regular whiteboard, or chart paper

Ask students to sit around you. Think of a historical period or a scientific concept that you have recently studied, and have a conversation about creating a story plan similar to this one:

Teacher: We have been studying about pioneer times. What were some of the struggles that pioneers faced?

[List student responses on the whiteboard or chart.]

Naomi: Their crops sometimes didn't grow because there wasn't enough rain.

Trevor: Many were homesick for their families back east.

Spencer: It was difficult to clear the land and build a house.

Cyd: Sometimes they had a hard time traveling through the mountains and across rivers.

Riley: Sometimes people got ill and died because there weren't any doctors or medicine.

Teacher: All of these certainly were real problems that the pioneers faced each and every day. Any one of these could be a good problem or job for a pioneer. Let's create a simple story plan around one of these concerns.

I've listed all five of your problems or jobs as you called them out. Let's pick one to be our problem for a possible story. Which of these could a character work toward and accomplish by the story's end?

[Select one student to make your choice.]

Cyd: Let's use the one where their covered wagon has to cross a river.

Teacher: That is a great problem for a story. Let's create the rest of the story plan.

[Write the word "Character" at the top of your board or chart paper.]

Teacher: We need to select a character for our story. Do you want it to be a girl or a boy who is helping the family cross the river?

[Again, always select one student to make these decisions quickly.]

Max: A boy.

Teacher: We need a name for our character—a name that is appropriate for that time. I'll take three suggestions.

Students: Jonathan; Benjamin; Samuel.

Literature Link

These picture books tell great stories that include accurate historical settings or scientific information.

- Camping With the President
  by Ginger Wadsworth
- Freedom School, Yes!
  by Amy Littlesugar
- A Good Night for Freedom
  by Barbara Olenyik Morrow
- Henry's Freedom Box
  by Ellen Levine
- Living Sunlight
  by Molly Bang & Penny Chisholm
- This Is Your Life Cycle
  by Heather Lynn Miller
- Trout Are Made of Trees
  by April Pulley Sayre

[*Ask one student to select the name of the character.*]

Leah: Samuel.

Teacher: How old is Samuel? Is he 7, 8, or 10 years old? [*Keep the age of the protagonist near the ages of the students.*]

Spencer: He is 8.

[*Write "boy," "Samuel," and "age 8" beside "Character."*]

Teacher: We already have our problem.

[*Write "Problem" beneath "Character."*]

Beside "Problem," I'll write "getting covered wagon across a river." Now we need a setting. The setting is both time and place. When might a river be running exceptionally strong or high?

Naomi: In the spring when the snow melts and it is raining.

Max: In the summer after a lot of heavy rains.

Teacher: Either of those could work. I'm going to select spring. What month or year would this be? Remember, we want to keep this as historically accurate as possible.

Students: April, 1851; May, 1850; March, 1849.

[*Call on one student to select one of the dates.*]

Mimi: May—the snow would be melting and there could be heavy rains. May, 1850.

[*Underneath "Problem," write "Setting" and "May, 1850."*]

Teacher: Now, where does this story take place? What river are Samuel and his family trying to cross? The place should add another layer of hard work and possible tension to the story.

Students: The Mississippi River; the Ohio River; the Missouri River.

[*Ask one student to make the choice.*]

Ellie: Let's use the Ohio River.

Teacher: I will add "Ohio River" after "May, 1850." Now we need to think about what will happen in this story. And we need to have some information— some real facts— about what the pioneers did when crossing a river. Some of our factual terms won't be in our plan, but they will appear in our story. For instance, we would want to use the correct terms for the wagon parts, for the kinds of animals that traveled with the pioneers, and for the food and supplies that they typically carried to their new homes.

[*Write "Events" on your story plan.*]

A story starts when something happens. So let's start this story at the river. What is Samuel doing?

Students: Sitting in the wagon; standing at the edge of the river and listening to the water rush by; helping his father empty the wagon of supplies.

Nonfiction Writing Lessons That Work © 2012 by Lola M. Schaefer, Scholastic Teaching Resources

Teacher: All good suggestions. Let's begin with "helping his father empty the wagon of supplies."

[Write #1 under "Events" and next to it write "Samuel—empty supplies—wagon." Always use reminder words on a story plan.]

Continue with this process until students have brainstormed three events, each of which decreases the family's chances of crossing the river. For the resolution, or ending, make sure your protagonist—Samuel in this case—does something that truly helps the wagon travel safely across the river.

Teacher: Here is our completed story plan. You worked hard. I'm going to put this up in the classroom so you can use it as an example if you choose to write your own science or social studies story to show what you know.

Character	boy—Samuel—age 8
Problem	getting covered wagon across a river
Setting	May, 1850, banks of the Ohio River
Events	#1 Samuel—helps empty supplies—wagon #2 Samuel helps father remove wheels— father injured #3 Samuel swims cattle to other side
Resolution	floats wagon on bottom—Samuel pushes with spike pole, avoids rocks—reaches other side

Self-Selected Characters and Problems for Story

After you have shared three or four informational stories with students, it's helpful to brainstorm some possible characters and problems for future writing.

Teacher: Who are some famous people that we've studied this year?

Students: Thomas Edison; John Cabot; Henry Hudson; Harriet Tubman; Rosa Parks.

Teacher:	Let's take one of those characters and see how we could put a story idea together.
	[*Ask one student to make a choice.*]
Omar:	Let's use Harriet Tubman.
Teacher:	Good choice. Now what kinds of problems or jobs could she have?
Ellie:	She could be signaling families that it's their night to escape.
Max:	She could be on the Underground Railroad and hurt herself.
Keisha:	She might be ill and have to hide from the slave catchers.
Teacher:	Any of these ideas would make a good problem for Harriet Tubman to solve. Now let's think about what we've been doing in science. Lately we've been studying different animal habitats. Name a few animals that you now know a lot about.
Students:	Penguins; owls; alligators; rattlesnakes; giraffes.
Teacher:	Let's select one of those as a character for a story.
	[*Ask one student to make a choice.*]
Spencer:	Owl.
Teacher:	What are some jobs that the owl would need to do, or what is a problem that a real owl would have in nature?
Leah:	Needs to build a nest.
Rogan:	It's losing its habitat and needs to move somewhere else.
Connor:	A bad storm blows the nest out of a tree, and a baby owl is left alone and struggling to survive.
Trevor:	A mature owl swoops down to snatch a chipmunk and gets caught in a snare.
Teacher:	All of these would make a good problem or job for the owl character.

I encourage you to brainstorm with your students several possible characters and what they need to do or how they are struggling. Remember that characters can be the moon, the sun, rain, or the woods, as well as people.

It's this kind of discussion and oral practice that shows students how to brainstorm characters and problems for their own informational stories. You might remind students that most problems revolve around the following:

- needing something

- avoiding danger

- constructing or building something

- feeling fearful

The Purpose Behind Story

Story provides students with a natural way to show what they know. They can create characters and place them in a situation that is true to life. Through the progression of the story, students can use terms and facts about the setting and the character's struggle. When they include factual content in a storyline, that information becomes relevant. Their stories show us that they know their information.

As with all stories, an informational story is meant to entertain. Students enjoy expressing themselves through story. The freedom to create characters and plots is appealing and fun. Story also appeals to the audience's imagination. For a few minutes, both writer and reader are transported to another place and time.

Process of Independent Writing

Students in grades 2–5 need a lot of practice in creating story plans. In fact, it's best to have students work together to create at least three or four story plans before expecting them to create a story on their own. With every example, make sure that something important happens during each event and that each example includes historical or scientific terms or references for factual accuracy. Once students have this foundation, they can create their own informational stories.

Process for Independent Writing
Review these story-writing steps with students:
✓ Brainstorm two or three topics that might lend themselves to a story.
✓ Select the one topic you know better than the others.
✓ Create a character.
✓ Brainstorm two or three different problems, struggles, or jobs for this character. Select the problem that will cause your character to work the hardest.
✓ Start your story with a significant event.
✓ Add at least three events that build the tension or conflict and push the character.
✓ Include accurate historical or scientific details to the events of the story.
✓ Write a resolution in which the character does something natural that will end the conflict or complete the job.

THE ELEMENTS OF CRAFT

Students practice the following elements of craft while writing informational story: focus, word choice, leads, endings, plotting, development of ideas and information, voice, organization, and conventions. You can design mini-lessons on any or all of these elements to improve the quality of student writing.

Story Titles

Some students like to have a working title for a story before they ever begin drafting. If that helps them focus and remain excited about what they're writing, encourage that. Most authors, though, wait until they have written the entire story before deciding on a title. That way, they can craft a title that will lure readers and listeners into the story.

One of the easiest ways to help students title their stories is by looking at several picture books. Select books that your students already know. Discuss how they think those authors probably decided on their titles. Here are some considerations to offer to your students:

- Do you want to use your character's name in the title?

- Find two or three places in your story where something important happens. Jot down a few of the nouns or verbs from those places. Would you like to use any of those words in your title?

- Avoid using any part of the ending in your title. The title needs to encourage your audience to read your story. If the reader already knows how it's going to end, why read it?

- Your title needs to match the tone of your story. If your story is humorous, your title should be a little funny. If your writing instills wonder and is gentle in nature, your title needs to show that, too.

- Usually, shorter titles work better than longer ones. Sometimes authors use longer titles to add humor or to exaggerate to make a certain point.

- Some authors like to use one-word titles. Is there one word that is important in your story that could make a strong title?

Fourth-Grade Story

A fourth-grade boy wrote this informational story after an independent study of leopards.

Where's My Leopard?

Hello. My name is Jimmy and I've lost my leopard. His name is Polkadots. He's a solitary leopard, which means he lives alone, except for me. I think he's mad at me because I didn't feed him his antelope this morning. He loves to eat mammals.

Polkadots usually stays around my house because he's afraid some poachers will shoot him. Poachers hunt animals illegally. Usually they want leopards for their beautiful coats. All leopards are spotted all over.

I bet Polkadots is thirsty. I better go look near our hose in the backyard. No! Not here! I just remembered that leopards can go for about a month without water. Oh well, nice try.

I think I've looked everywhere. He couldn't be hiding anywhere that's small because he is (and most leopards are) 40–50 inches from the head to the end of the back. By the way, that's not counting his long tail.

He can probably hear me right now. His hearing is very keen. It's twice the range that humans have. Why, he can probably hear me snap my fingers when he's all the way over in the neighbor's yard. I've got the best leopard in the whole world. I just wish I could find him.

I bet you're wondering how I got a leopard since they live in most of Africa and throughout Asia. My uncle lives over there. He sent Polkadots to me. Weird, huh?

I thought he might be hiding in the basement because basements are like lairs to a leopard, but mostly only the female leopards live in lairs. That's where they take care of their cubs.

I just thought of something. Polkadots could be hiding in the bushes or grass. After all, his polka-dots camouflage him. Oh! I just saw some scratches on a tree. That's how leopards mark their territory. He must be somewhere in my backyard.

There he is! He was hiding in a tree the whole time! I should have known. Leopards spend most of their day in trees! I don't need your help anymore. I've found my leopard.

This story has a character with a problem. It also includes quite a bit of information about leopards. It is a strong example of informational story.

Audience /Feedback

Whether your students share their stories within the classroom, visit another classroom to read them, or take them home and ask for written feedback from parents and friends, they need to have a focused purpose for someone to read or listen to their story. Writers always appreciate feedback—specific feedback on what the audience found exciting, creative, unique, or humorous about their story. It's what fuels us to write more and to write better.

Here are some suggested prompts for eliciting audience feedback:

- *Did you hear scientific or historical information in this story? What are some examples that you remember?*

- *Did the character work at his job or at solving a problem? How?*

- *When you heard my title, what did you think this story was about?*

- *Can you retell what happened in the story?*

- *Were there any terms or facts that you particularly enjoyed?*

 Nonfiction Writing Lessons That Work © 2012 by Lola M. Schaefer, Scholastic Teaching Resources

CHAPTER 8

Show Factual Information Through Riddles

Writing riddles can show students' knowledge and understanding of a topic because it requires them to present different aspects of a particular subject in the form of clues. Whether riddles are written in prose form or as poems, they engage both writer and audience from the first line to the last. Students will tell you that the best part of writing riddles is reading them—and having an audience guess the answer.

Exploring Riddles

Materials: *When Riddles Come Rumbling* by Rebecca Kai Dotlich or other books of riddles

Begin by reading three or four riddles to your students and having them guess the answers. Then go back and reread one of the riddles again. In the model below, I use the poem-riddle about a snake from *When Riddles Come Rumbling* by Rebecca Kai Dotlich.

Teacher: What clues in the riddle led you to your answer?

Students: "A hisssss"; "I speak in reptile-tongue"; "I curl"; "I garden-glide"; "I misssssssss."

Teacher: Let's look at this poem-riddle and count the different clues.

[Students should be able to identify nine or ten clues, depending on how they interpret the lines.]

Let's look at the first two clues: "curl" and "coil." Did you think it was a snake yet?

Students: No.

Teacher: The author's next clues talk about sliding, slinking, and gliding. Did you know it was a snake yet?

Students:	No; I knew it was some kind of animal; I thought it was an animal that stayed on the ground.
Teacher:	Her next clue was "reptile-tongue." What did that make you think it was?
Students:	A lizard; a snake.
Teacher:	What confirmed your guesses?
Students:	"Hisssssss and misssssss."
Teacher:	So, in this poem-riddle, the author starts with clues that don't give it away immediately, and the clues get more specific to "snake" as the poem continues.

Study one or two more poems in this manner with students. We always look at the poem-riddle about licorice in *When Riddles Come Rumbling*. This licorice poem-riddle has some red herrings—some lines that tell readers what the candy doesn't have: It doesn't have feet, thumbs, or toes. After solving the riddle, we discuss how these false clues are true statements that make it a tad bit more confusing. These facts tend to throw the reader off track for a moment or two.

> *Literature Link*
>
> *These books contain riddles that provide good models for student writing:*
> - *Arithme-Tickle by J. Patrick Lewis*
> - *Scien-Trickery by J. Patrick Lewis*
> - *Spot the Plot by J. Patrick Lewis*
> - *When Riddles Come Rumbling by Rebecca Kai Dotlich*

Writing an Informational Riddle

Materials: an interactive whiteboard, a regular whiteboard, or chart paper; paper and pencils

To begin, ask students to sit around you.

Teacher:	Who are some of the famous people that we have been studying?
Students:	Harriet Tubman; Frederick Douglass; Paul Revere; Rosa Parks; Ben Franklin.
Teacher:	We could write an informational riddle about one of those people, or we could write a riddle about another topic that we have been studying in social studies, or in science or math. What are some other topics?
Students:	Multiplication; giraffes; habitats; branches of the government; rocks and minerals; simple machines; weather; amphibians.
Teacher:	Any of these topics would work.
	[*Point to one student and give him or her three specific topic choices.*]
	Would you like to write an information riddle about Harriet Tubman, hurricanes, or a frog?
Roberto:	Harriet Tubman.
	[*Write responses so everyone can easily see the development of the riddle.*]

Teacher: What are some clues—short phrases—that we could use for Harriet Tubman? These clues could be the names of people or places or terms from that time, anything that helped Harriet Tubman do her job. Since this is informational writing, the clues must all be true, or factual.

Students: Underground Railroad; slaves to freedom; walking at night; safe houses; follow the stars; Maryland; Pennsylvania; Moses; abolitionists; slave catchers.

Teacher: What a great list of important words, terms, and names to help describe Harriet Tubman. I've been writing these reminder words down the right side of the board. Please copy these words down on the right side of your sheet of paper.

[When you've completed a list of clues, it will look like this:

Underground Railroad

slaves to freedom

walking at night

safe houses

follow the stars

Maryland—Pennsylvania

Moses

abolitionists

slave catchers]

Teacher: We are now ready to write our riddle. It can be written in prose or as a poem.

[Call on one student.]

Would you like to write this riddle as a poem or as a regular riddle in sentences?

Ellie: In sentences.

Teacher: Do you want to write the riddle as if you are Harriet Tubman, or as someone describing Harriet Tubman?

Max: As if we are Harriet Tubman.

Teacher: Let's begin. Study your reminder words. Which clue can we use to begin our riddle that will not give away who we're thinking about? We also want it to be a little intriguing, like a lure, so the audience will want to continue to read.

Sachi: Come with me and walk in the night.

Teacher: That's a great first line. Thank you. Let's write that first line on the left side of our paper. Now, look at your clues again. Select another clue that will provide information about Harriet Tubman without giving away her identity. For instance, we don't want to mention slaves and freedom or the Underground Railroad just yet.

Liam: Don't talk, and keep your heads low. I will guide you to a safe house.

Teacher: That's wonderful. You are painting a great picture. Let's add those two sentences to our riddle. It's a good idea to have five or six clues for your reader. What do you want to mention next?

Naomi: The abolitionists are my friends. The slave catchers are my enemies.

Teacher: You've given strong information in those two sentences. Let's add those clues to our riddle. We only need two more clues, but you can add more. I have crossed out the clues in the right column that you have already used. You might want to do that on your sheet of paper as well. And let's read what we have written so far. That will help us know what we want to add.

> *Come with me and walk in the night. Don't talk and keep your heads low. I will guide you to a safe house. The abolitionists are my friends. The slave catchers are my enemies.*

Again, look at our reminder words. We still don't want to give away the answer. Which clue would you like to add now?

Spencer: Look up. Follow the stars north—north to freedom.

Teacher: I am adding those two sentences. Write them on your paper, too. I think you're ready for one last clue.

Cyd: I am called Moses and I will help you be free.

Omar: Or, you are now a part of the Underground Railroad.

Roberto: Or, let me lead you to the Underground Railroad.

Teacher: Any of these final clues would be excellent. Why don't you decide and write the ending that you think is most appropriate? I'm going to add this to my riddle: "I am called Moses and I will help you be free."

To end our riddles, let's write, "Who am I?" That way our audience will know to respond.

Here is our final riddle—although your next-to-last line may be different from this one:

> *Come with me and walk in the night. Don't talk, and keep your heads low. I will guide you to a safe house. The abolitionists are my friends. The slave catchers are my enemies. Look up. Follow the stars north— north to freedom. I am called Moses and I will help you be free. Who am I?*

Count how many different clues you gave the audience in your riddle. Now you are ready to write riddles on your own.

 Nonfiction Writing Lessons That Work © 2012 by Lola M. Schaefer, Scholastic Teaching Resources

Self-Selected Topics for Informational Riddles

There is an unlimited supply of topics for informational riddles. Some students enjoy writing riddles about different kinds of punctuation. Some prefer to do what J. Patrick Lewis does in *Spot the Plot*, writing riddles for book titles or characters in well-known children's literature. Your students might want to write a riddle about a picture book or chapter book. This kind of riddle would also make a great literature response.

If your students study explorers, inventors, presidents, or statesmen, they might enjoy showing what they know by writing a riddle. I've seen students write riddles about specific battles, forms of precipitation, weapons of the Civil War, and weather instruments. Of course, riddles about more general topics, such as animals, landforms, seed-bearing plants, geometric shapes, and different body parts, show what students know as well.

If your students record ideas in a writer's notebook, they will enjoy keeping a section for topics that could become riddles. It's also advisable to have your students copy a sample riddle in their notebook as a reference for structure.

Student Riddles

Here are a few riddles written by third-grade students who were studying different forms of energy and its uses.

I use lots
of sun energy
I have no feet
I don't talk
I make energy
I am flat
and big
I save lots of electricity
I help save the earth.
What am I?

(solar panel)

by Emerson

I use energy every day.
I
hang
from
your
ceiling
and break easily.
I am hot
when you touch me.
I stop working
after a while.
I am small and round.
What am I?

(a light bulb)

by Hayden

continued on next page

Student Riddles, *continued . . .*

These riddles are by fourth-grade students who had just completed a study of explorers.

1609 was my big year,	In 1609
for I set off without any fear.	my journey began
Hudson River was where I went,	an English explorer
but then there was quite	hired to search for a Passage
an event.	and found myself
Ice covered all the sea,	at a different place
then everyone turned to me.	now known as a bay
They didn't care that I was	named after me
captain,	stuck in the cold
for I was off	for the entire winter
before I knew what had	but then set adrift
happened.	by my unhappy crew
Who am I?	Who am I?
(Henry Hudson)	(Henry Hudson)
by Ethan Pope	*by Clara Dillon*

The Purpose Behind Information Riddles

When students write, we want them engaged in thinking about the topic, in writing, and in sharing with an audience to elicit purposeful feedback. Riddles supply a structure that satisfies all these requirements. It is also a kind of informational writing that can be demonstrated in a short amount of time. Students quickly learn the steps needed to write riddles and can easily write their own in one language arts period, or during science, social studies, or math.

Process for Independent Writing

Make sure that your collaborative prewrite and informational riddle are on display to support students as they write their own riddles. They can also open their writers' notebook and follow the step-by-step approach in the examples they've copied down.

Nonfiction Writing Lessons That Work © 2012 by Lola M. Schaefer, Scholastic Teaching Resources

Process for Independent Writing

Review the steps for writing informational riddles with students:

✓ Select a topic that you know well.

✓ Decide whether to write your riddle in prose or as a poem.

✓ List at least seven to nine different clues down the right side of your paper with just one or two reminder words.

✓ Select a clue to begin the riddle that is general or vague, yet factual. Write it on the left side of your paper.

✓ Continue adding four or five more factual clues, getting more specific toward the end of the riddle.

✓ End the riddle with one of the following questions: *Who am I? What am I? Who is it? What is it?*

THE ELEMENTS OF CRAFT

Students practice the following elements of craft while writing informational riddles: focus, word choice, details, voice, and sometimes conventions. You can design mini-lessons, on any or all of these elements, to improve the quality of student writing.

Audience/Feedback

Students who write informational riddles will want to read them to an audience. Sharing writing usually only happens in our own classroom, but since riddles are short and fun, it works out well to allow a few students to visit another classroom for a "Riddle Break." One student introduces the riddle reading by explaining why the class was writing riddles and what response is expected from the audience. After each riddle, listeners have an opportunity to guess the answer.

Another way to share riddles is to post them in the hall without the answers. Instead, hang an empty sheet of paper at the bottom of each riddle and encourage readers to write their guesses.

Riddles are solved by putting the different clues together. Below are some questions that writers can pose to their audiences to foster this process. Suggest to your students that they only ask one or two of these questions after the riddle has been solved.

- *Which factual clue(s) helped you solve the riddle?*

- *Which facts did you put together to solve the riddle?*

- *Did any of the clues confuse you or throw you off?*

- *Can you think of another factual clue that could have been used for this topic or person?*

Bibliography

Aliki. (1999). *William Shakespeare & the Globe*. New York: HarperCollins.

Aston, D. H. (2006). *An egg is quiet*. San Francisco: Chronicle Books.

Aston, D. H. (2007). *A seed is sleepy*. San Francisco: Chronicle Books.

Bang, M., & Chisholm, P. (2009). *Living sunlight: How plants bring the earth to life*. New York: Blue Sky Press.

Barretta, G. (2006). *Now & Ben: The modern inventions of Benjamin Franklin*. New York: Henry Holt.

Barretta, G. *Neo Leo: The ageless ideas of Leonardo da Vinci*. New York: Henry Holt.

Baylor, B. (1972). *When clay sings*. New York: Aladdin Books.

Collard, S. B., III. (1997). *Animal dads*. Boston: Houghton Mifflin.

Collard, S. B., III. (2008). *Teeth*. Watertown, MA: Charlesbridge.

Cox, R. (1996). *Pigs peek*. Katonah, NY: Richard C. Owen Publishers.

Dotlich, R. K. (2001). *When riddles come rumbling*. Honesdale, PA: Boyds Mills Press.

Duke, N. (2003). *Reading to learn from the very beginning: Information books in early childhood*. National Association for the Education of Young Children. Retrieved November 18, 2011, from www.naeyc.org/files/yc/file/200303/InformationBooks.pdf.

Florian, D. (1997). *in the swim*. San Diego: Harcourt Brace.

Franco, B. (2009). *Pond circle*. New York: Margaret K. McElderry Books.

Hopkins, L. B. (2006). *Got geography!* New York: Greenwillow Books.

Hopkins, L. B. (1999). *Lives: Poems about famous Americans*. New York: HarperCollins.

Hopkins, L. B. (1999). *Spectacular science*. New York: Simon & Schuster.

Jenkins, S., & Page, R. (2010). *How to clean a hippopotamus*. New York: Houghton Mifflin.

Lewis, J. P. (2002). *Arithme-Tickle*. San Diego: Houghton Mifflin Harcourt.

Lewis, J. P. (2004). *Scien-Trickery*. San Diego: Houghton Mifflin Harcourt.

Lewis, J. P. (2009). *Spot the plot*. San Francisco: Chronicle Books.

Levine, E. (2007). *Henry's freedom box: A true story from the Underground Railroad*. New York: Scholastic.

Littlesugar, A. (2001). *Freedom school, yes!* New York: Philomel.

Martin, J. B. (1998). *Snowflake Bentley*. Boston: Houghton Mifflin.

McMillan, B. (1993). *Puffins climb, penguins rhyme*. San Diego: Harcourt.

Miller, H. L. (2008). *This is your life cycle*. New York: Clarion.

Morrow, B. O. (2004). *A good night for freedom*. New York: Holiday House.

Peters, L. W. (2003). *Earthshake: Poems from the ground up*. New York: Greenwillow.

Ryan, P. M. (1996). *The flag we love*. Watertown, MA: Charlesbridge.

Sayre, A. P. (2010). *Meet the howlers*. Watertown, MA: Charlesbridge.

Sayre, A. P. (2008). *Trout are made of trees*. Watertown, MA: Charlesbridge.

Schaefer, L. (2006). *An island grows*. New York: Greenwillow.

Sis, P. (2004). *The train of states*. New York: Greenwillow.

St. George, J. (2002). *So you want to be an inventor?* New York: Philomel.

St. George, J. (2000). *So you want to be President?* New York: Philomel.

Swinburne, S. R. (1999). *Unbeatable beaks*. New York: Henry Holt.

Wadsworth, G. (2009). *Camping with the President*. Honesdale, PA: Boyds Mills Press.

Wick, W. (1997). *A drop of water*. New York: Scholastic.